NORTH AMERICAN
BIRDS
— OF —
PREY

NORTH AMERICAN
BIRDS
— OF —
PREY

SCOTT WEIDENSAUL

LEFT Bald Eagle

GALLERY BOOKS
An Imprint of W. H. Smith Publishers Inc.
112 Madison Avenue
New York City 10016

A QUINTET BOOK
produced for
GALLERY BOOKS
An imprint of W.H. Smith Publishers Inc.
112 Madison Avenue
New York, New York 10016

ISBN 0-8317-6425-2

This book was designed and produced by
Quintet Publishing Limited
6 Blundell Street
London N7 8BH

Creative Director: Peter Bridgewater
Art Director: Ian Hunt
Editor: Judith Simons

Typeset in Great Britain by
Central Southern Typesetters, Eastbourne
Manufactured in Hong Kong by
Leefung-Asco Printers Limited

All photographs supplied by

VIREO

Visual Resources for Ornithology

CONTENTS

INTRODUCTION

Raptors, such as this Swainson's hawk eating a vole, are adapted for a life of hunting and killing, with powerful, taloned feet for grabbing prey, and hooked beaks for tearing meat.

A young great horned owl, out of the nest but still unable to fly, already has the majestic mien of its imposing parents. Great horneds are the most widely distributed raptor in the Western Hemisphere.

*F*or as long as mankind has had an imagination, birds of prey have had an exalted place in it. And little wonder – who hasn't stood breathless at the sight of a hawk arrowing through the air, as if earth and sky were at its command, or felt their hackles rise at the midnight hoot of an unseen owl?

But what is a bird of prey? Not simply a bird that kills other animals; by that criteria, a robin eating a worm, or a loon catching a fish, would qualify. Actually, the better term is "raptor," which refers to those predatory birds that have evolved specialized beaks and talons used to catch their food.

Raptors, then, include the hawks, eagles, falcons and owls; vultures are usually included in the roll on account of close relation, even though they do not kill their own food. In North America, some 52 species of raptors can be found on a regular basis – three vultures, 23 hawks and eagles, seven falcons and 19 owls. They run

Red-tailed hawks (like this youngster, still with a brown tail) are buteos, members of the group of soaring hawks that ride thermal air currents while hunting or migrating.

The golden eagle of the West and Canada is an active hunter of rabbits, marmots and other mammals. This is an immature bird, which will lose the white wing patches and tail band as it matures.

the gamut from the California condor, with its 9-foot wingspan, to the sparrow-sized elf owl of the Southwestern deserts. Some eat only birds, some only fish, some only mice. One eats only a particular species of snail. The great horned owl, on the other hand, will eat almost anything from the size of a raccoon or a skunk on down.

Obviously, with such a range of lifestyles, raptors show many different forms, but they all share a few common features. The beak is invariably hooked and sharp, to tear food into bite-sized chunks for swallowing. The feet are strong, with sharp, curved talons (vultures being the exception.) All have excellent eyesight, with the eyes in the front of the head, affording binocular vision for better depth perception – crucial for chasing and capturing lively prey. Most are good fliers, although this trait is not universal; many owls are weak fliers, and hunt from perches, only swooping down when prey is spotted.

Vultures – Naked heads and the ability to soar for hours mark the three species of vultures – the turkey vulture, black vulture and California condor. The lack of face and neck feathers is an evolutionary nod toward cleanliness, since these birds spend a great deal of time with their heads stuck in some very messy places and it is easier to wipe bare skin clean than feathers. Their feet are relatively weak, and instead of talons they have blunt, ineffectual claws.

Buteos are the soaring hawks, with wide tails and broad wings to catch rising columns of air called thermals, and this group includes

some of the most widespread and best-known of raptors. With 12 North American species, this is also the largest group on the continent, and includes the red-tailed hawk (common in open country over most of the U.S. and Canada,) the red-shouldered hawk of moist forests, and the ferruginous hawk of the Plains.

Accipiters are agile, forest-dwelling hawks that eat primarily birds. There are three species, very similar except for size, with rounded wings for short bursts of speed, and long tails for excellent maneuverability. The sharp-shinned hawk is jay-sized, the goshawk crow-sized, and the Cooper's hawk in the middle.

The four species of **kites** are small, buoyant hawks, primarily southern and western in distribution. Most are delicately built, with long pointed wings and a diet heavy on insects and rodents, although the snail kite of south Florida eats (naturally enough) snails.

The **northern harrier** is the only North American representative of a genus found over much of the world. A hunter of mice, the harrier drifts low over fields on long, narrow wings. A pronounced facial disc – like that of an owl – allows the harrier to hunt by ear, for the peculiar ruff that surrounds the face funnels sound.

Although similar in size, the continent's two **eagles** – the bald and the golden – are not alike in lifestyle. The golden is built like a

American kestrels are the most widespread and common of North America's falcons. Only the size of a mourning dove, the kestrel nonetheless has the tapered wings and long tail of its larger cousins.

Among the owl's adaptations for night hunting are large, light-sensitive eyes, soft wing feathers for silent flight, and exceptional hearing. The "ear" tufts on this long-eared owl are simply camouflaging feathers, however – the actual ear openings are hidden beneath the facial discs.

giant *buteo*, and is a superb hunter of rabbits and other medium-sized mammals. The bald eagle, while capable of hunting, prefers to take carrion or fish, and leads a rather more sedentary existence.

The **osprey** is one of the most unusual raptors. Found throughout much of the world, including most of North America, the osprey is a fish-eating specialist that dives into the water from great heights for its prey. In flight, a crooked "gull wing" profile is distinctive; from below, the osprey's wings are very long and narrow.

Every line of a **falcon's** body is built for speed, from its scimitar wings to its long tail and streamlined form. There are six species, including the peregrine falcon, revered by falconers and the fastest living thing on earth, capable of dives of 175 mph. More common is the American kestrel, a dove-sized falcon that hunts mice and insects in farmland. The caracara of the South, although classified with the falcons, looks nothing like one; it is a long-legged bird more reminiscent of a vulture than the fleet-winged falcons.

The **barn-owl**, like the osprey, is found almost worldwide. Because of many anatomical differences, it is classified separately from the other owls, which are referred to as **true owls**. This

A female kestrel delivers a morsel of food to her nest, an abandoned woodpecker hole in a pine tree. Kestrels will accept artificial nest boxes, an easy way to increase the population of these colorful hawks.

category includes all the rest of North America's night hunters, from the massive great gray owl on down to the elf and pygmy-owls. Barn-owls and true owls, even though they apparently arose from different ancestral stock, have evolved similar adaptations for night hunting – excellent hearing (enhanced by their facial ruffs,) acute night vision and near-silent flight, thanks to downy edges on the major flight feathers.

THE VALUE OF PREDATION

People may admire raptors for their beauty and grace, but that has never stopped us from resenting them with great enthusiasm, too. Through the centuries, birds of prey have been reviled as compet-

While her chicks try to hide from the photographer, a female osprey delivers a fish to the nest, built on a platform erected in a saltmarsh. Ospreys have made a strong recovery along the East Coast, after pesticides threatened their existence in the 1960s.

itors for food and game, as heartless butchers, even as a danger to human life.

Only in the past century have we begun to understand the valuable role that predators, including hawks and owls, play in the balance of nature. Far from being a threat to the species upon which they play, predators are essential for their well-being. Predators, because they generally take the easiest prey, weed out the weak, ill and genetically defective, leaving the strong to carry on the species. Large plant-eaters, like moose and deer, can even over-populate their habitat if not controlled by predators. The situation is somewhat different for smaller animals like mice, which exist in vast numbers that not even their predators can dent, but it is clear that raptors are internal cogs in the complex natural mechanism that has evolved over millions of years.

Legal protection for raptors was late in coming. Decades after songbirds and other native species were placed the list of protected species, hawks and owls were still fair game, and even bald and golden eagles were the targets of bounties. That lamentable situation began to change after World War II, and today all raptors enjoy full *protection under federal, state and provincial law, with hefty fines and jail sentences for those that kill them.*

While the threat of illegal shooting has not disappeared, the hazards facing raptors today are far more insidious. Habitat loss is perhaps the most pressing; from spotted owls in the Pacific Northwest to snail kites in the Everglades, birds of prey are endangered when the land they need is destroyed or altered. Chemical toxins have also taken a heavy toll. Widespread use of DDT and other so-called "hard" pesticides almost wiped out the bald eagle, osprey and peregrine falcon in the 1950s and '60s, and although the most persistent insecticides have been banned in the U.S., they are still manufactured here and sold abroad, often contaminating the same birds on their wintering grounds. Neither are the legal pesticides harmless. Carbofuran, commonly used on corn, has been implicated in the deaths of thousands of birds, including raptors.

There is reason for optimism, though. Education and a growing environmental awareness have tipped the scales in the raptors' favour, at least for now. Many birders are discovering that they can also help directly, by erecting nesting boxes for cavity-users like screech-owls and kestrels and artificial nest platforms for ospreys, by volunteering for migration counts or censuses like the wintering eagle survey conducted each year by the National Wildlife Federation, by helping at raptor education centers and refuges. In a sense, it is a way of giving something back to the birds for the excitement and beauty they can give to us.

A peregrine falcon guards its nest, nothing more than a scrape on a windswept Alaskan river bluff. Peregrine populations in the Lower 48 plummeted due to insecticide contamination, and they are only now returning to their former haunts thanks to captive breeding and reintroduction programs.

OBSERVING RAPTORS

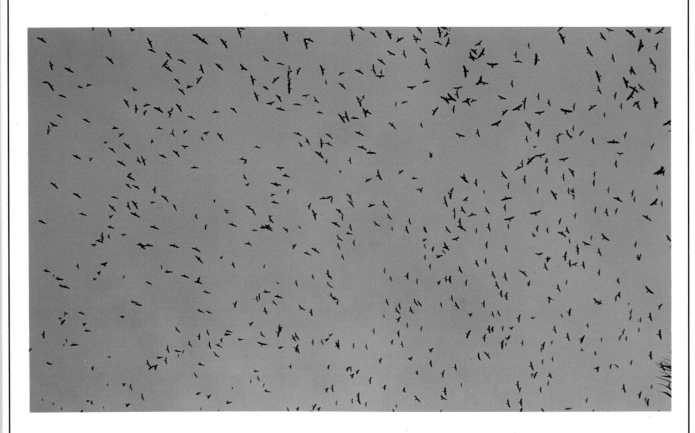

Hundreds of broad-winged hawks wheel in a massive thermal in Panama, on their way from the eastern U.S. and Canada to their South American wintering grounds.

*F*rom the ridges of Pennsylvania and the New Jersey coast to bluffs that overlook the Great Lakes and the mountains of the American West, watching raptors is one of the fastest-growing forms of birding. Hawk-watching in particular attracts thousands of new converts each year, while others enjoy the challenge of tracking down owls.

WATCHING HAWKS

Hawk-watching is primarily a spring and fall sport, and was pioneered at Hawk Mountain Sanctuary, along the Kittatinny Ridge in eastern Pennsylvania. Here, hawks, falcons and eagles heading south in the fall concentrate along the mountaintop, passing close by a rocky outcropping where thousands of visitors train their binoculars on the passing parade. Since the sanctuary's founding in 1934, annual migration counts have been kept, and identification techniques have been honed. It is not unusual for an experienced observer to identify a hawk when it is still nearly a mile away, going by color, shape and behavior.

Peregrine falcons are primarily coastal migrants, so the best places to catch a glimpse of this endangered species are sites like Cape May, N.J., where a peninsula jutting into Delaware Bay concentrates the flight.

Since the 1930s, many other observation points have been discovered, usually where some feature of geography concentrates the migration. One of the best is Cape May, New Jersey, a peninsula that juts south into Delaware Bay. Hawks (and at night, owls) moving south funnel to the Cape's point before striking off across the bay, sometimes in astounding numbers. This is one of the best places to see coastal migrants like peregrine falcons, merlins and osprey, but the Cape does not get the numbers of red-tailed hawks, goshawks and golden eagles that inland points can expect.

The fall migration follows a predictable schedule. Along the inland ridges, where the migration has been studied the longest, the flight begins in the humid days of mid-August, with a few bald eagles moving south; these are southern birds that, having finished

In many parts of the continent, especially the West, roadside hawk-watching can be very profitable. Hawks, like this adult ferruginous, like to use utility poles and isolated trees as hunting perches, and a slow approach in a car (which acts as a blind) may allow a close look.

breeding in early spring, "vacationed" in the North. By the first week of September the pace picks up dramatically, as more bald eagles, ospreys and broad-winged hawks begin to fly. The broad-winged peak usually comes in the second or third week of the month, with tens of thousands of these small buteos migrating.

The broad-winged flight ends abruptly, and by the last week in September and the beginning of October, the stage is held by the first good numbers of sharp-shinned hawks, which peak around the middle of October. At the same time, the greatest variety of raptors are migrating – red-shouldered hawks, peregrines, merlins, American kestrels, Cooper's hawks, northern harriers, ospreys and a few red-tails, golden eagles, rough-legged hawks and goshawks. These last four species move to the forefront by November, along with a second surge of bald eagles, this time those that breed in New England and Canada.

Fall hawk migrations are closely tied to the wind. In the East, both on the coast and along the ridges, the best flights usually come a day or two after the passage of a cold front, when the wind blows strong from the northwest. The blustery winds provide updrafts when they strike the hills or dunes, giving the hawks energy-saving lift.

Hawk migration has been little studied in the West, where isolated mountain systems make cross-country flights a more attractive option. At the few hawk lookouts in the West, sharp-shinned and Cooper's hawks, kestrel and red-tailed hawks are the main migrants, and days of southwest wind and approaching low pressure systems seem to be the best.

During the spring, hawks and eagles do not use the ridges and coast to the same degree as in fall, moving north instead on a broad front. Because there are few concentration points the spring migration is not well understood, although there are a growing number of places, like Sandy Hook in northern New Jersey, Whitefish Point Bird Observatory in Michigan's Upper Peninsula, Grimsby in Ontario and Braddock Bay State Park in New York, where organized hawk counts are taken during the spring.

Hawk identification can be difficult for the beginner. Many species, like the accipiters, are confusingly alike, and the distances involved make it hard to see conventional field marks. A good field guide is a help, but the best way to learn hawk identification is by

A red-tailed hawk rides a stiff autumn wind past a hawk-watch in New Jersey, one of many lookouts along the ridges of the East. Red-tails are late migrants, with the heaviest flights coming in late October and November.

going to an established lookout and talking to those who have been watching hawks for years. A single day with an expert is better than all the field guides in the world.

Watching Owls

Because of their nocturnal habits, owls are difficult to see, and finding one is usually a stroke of luck that comes when the birder is searching for something else. But more and more birders are making owls their speciality, and are learning that it is possible to stack the odds in one's favor.

Migratory patterns of western hawks, like this young Swainson's, are only now being studied. It is an area of ornithology to which knowledgeable amateurs can contribute a great deal.

With its habit of nesting in prairie towns, golf courses and woodlots, the Mississippi kite is one of the easily observed raptors on the U.S. Plains.

As hard as owls may be to see, they are easy to hear. Almost all of North America's 19 species have distinct calls that can be identified without ever seeing the bird. More importantly, most owls will respond to a tape recording of their species call, and may even fly close enouth to see, thinking the recording is an intruding owl.

Screech-owls, great horned owls and barred owls are among the easiest species to call in; sometimes even a good vocal imitation will suffice. A tape recording is more reliable, however. Owling tapes are now on the market, but for most people it is easier to tape from a bird-song record, like the excellent Peterson Field Guide to Bird Song, or the Guide to Bird Sounds from the National Geographic Society.

Calm, moonlit nights are the best for owling, and the hours after midnight seem to be somewhat better. Be sure to play the right call in the correct habitat – there is no point in calling for saw-whet owls in farm woodlots, or for screech-owls in northern bogs. Also, play the calls of the smallest owls first, because the sound of a great horned or barred owl (which would gladly prey on the smaller species) will frighten a screech-owl into silence. Play the call several times at medium volume, then wait for an answer.

A snowy owl takes wing across a northern New Jersey field, within sight of the New York City skyline. Northern owls like snowies sometimes wander south in the winter, affording an unusual opportunity for southern bird-watchers.

Watch the sky for the silhouette of the approaching owl; while great horned owls rarely come close, screech, barred and saw-whets will often perch in the trees nearby.

Using taped calls is disruptive to the owl's life, and must be used sparingly. During the courtship and breeding season – roughly February through July – tapes should be avoided completely, since they draw the owls away from caring for their young, and may even cause them to abandon their territory. At other times of the year, use restraint by not calling the same owls repeatedly, or for more than a few minutes.

Because owls eat their prey whole, or in large chunks, they must find a way to void the bones and other indigestibles that they swallow with the meat. They do so by coughing up a small pellet of

The broad-winged hawk provides some of the most exciting hawk-watching of the year, as hundreds of thousands pour south in September, migrating in large flocks known as kettles.

fur and bone each day. Because they usually pass their pellets while on roost, it is possible to find large numbers of them in one place. The presence of pellets is obviously a tip-off that a nest or winter roost is nearby, but the pellets themselves are an interesting facet of owl biology. Containing the remains of almost everything the owl eats, the pellets provide a clear record of local owl food habits. It is impossible to identify the species of owl strictly from the pellet, although large owls usually pass larger pellets, but by carefully scouting the area it may be possible to spot the owl itself.

The pellets will be dry and friable, coming apart in a mass of fur. Most will contain rodent bones, and with a good mammal field guide it is possible to pinpoint the kind of vole, mouse or shrew that was eaten. It is a fascinating exercise in field research that anyone can participate in.

Some owls migrate, but because they do so at night, the flights are impossible to watch – with one intriguing exception. At Cape May, N.J., where migrating owls are mist-netted for banding, the New Jersey Audubon Society conducts night-time owl watches at the base of the Cape May Lighthouse. Barn-owls, long-eared owls and saw-whet owls pass through the Cape's bottleneck, and appear as brief flashes in the revolving lighthouse beam – a riveting natural spectacle.

Crows harass a barn-owl taking a rare daytime flight. At least some barn-owls migrate south each fall, but because the flights take place at night, virtually nothing is known about this phase of their lives.

FROM BLACK VULTURE
TO BALD EAGLE

A SPECIES DIRECTORY OF BIRDS OF PREY

LEFT Northern Goshawk

BLACK VULTURE
CORAGYPS ATRATUS

Sporting a tail so short it almost merges with the trailing edges of the wings (leading to the nickname "the flying wing" among birders), the black vulture is a common scavenger in the South, where its hunched form is a fixture at garbage dumps and farms.

But while this species' stronghold is still south of the Mason-Dixon line, it has recently begun a surprising northward expansion. Black vultures now breed in Pennsylvania and New Jersey, and have been spotted as far north as New England – and they show no signs of slowing down. The reason for this sudden range shift remains a mystery, especially considering that black vultures are declining in many parts of their traditional home, but it serves as a reminder that bird populations are dynamic, not static.

With a wingspan of about 4½ feet, the black is the smallest of North America's three vultures. At rest it is pure ebony, with a wrinkled, dark gray head. In flight the solid black is relieved by a white patch at the end of each wing – a handy field mark if the light is right, but useless when one is looking at a silhouetted bird. It is better to differentiate the black vulture by its flat soaring profile and short tail, compared with the turkey vulture's pronounced dihedral and longer tail.

Black vultures nest in tree cavities, hollow logs, stumps and on the ground in dense vegetation. They occasionally breed in loose colonies, and the chicks stay with the parents through most of the following year, learning the best areas to hunt. Two eggs are the norm, but unfortunately they do not always hatch; eggshell thinning – the same pesticide-related problem that plagued the bald eagle and peregrine falcon – still afflicts black vultures, a malady that some blame for regional declines in black vulture numbers.

IDENTIFICATION

PLUMAGE: All black, with gray head and white wing patches.

DISTRIBUTION: Mid Atlantic, South and lower Midwest.

FOOD: Carrion.

NEST: Builds none; eggs laid on ground or stump.

EGGS: 2; white with brownish scrawls and wreathing.

Black vulture: adult

TURKEY VULTURE
CATHARTES AURA

Drifting on up-tilted wings through the sultry air of a summer afternoon, a turkey vulture rocks gently from side to side as it circles inside a thermal, a column of sun-warmed air rising from the land below. By catching thermals, a vulture can stay aloft for hours with scarcely a flap of its nearly six-foot wings, soaring over the countryside, watching for a likely meal. That meal may be big, like a road-killed deer, or small, like a dead catfish bloating in the sun – but it must be dead, for the turkey vulture has little truck with the living.

Known simply (and incorrectly) as a "buzzard" to most people, the turkey vulture is North America's aerial cleanup artist. Using sight and smell to locate its food, the vulture shows no hesitation about feeding on the rankest carrion, although it does display a preference for fresh food, if a choice is offered. The vulture's beak is strong and hooked, and although its feet do not have sharp talons, they make a sturdy brace for pulling chunks of meat free. Within half an hour, a single vulture can reduce a rabbit to a pile of empty skin – and the skin usually goes down the hatch at the end, too.

As repulsive as their eating habits may be, a turkey vulture in the air is a creature of grace. The wings are held in a shallow V, showing the dark body and wing linings against the silvery-gray primaries and secondaries. The head is naked and red (gray in young birds), but that feature can be surprisingly hard to see on a bird in flight, even in good light. The birds congregate at communal roosts each night, usually in the branches of a large, dead tree. At dawn they can be seen, wings outstretched to dry the dew, presenting a vaguely medieval tableau, like gargoyles on a cathedral.

The turkey vulture is common over most of the U.S., except for northern New England; it barely crosses

the Canadian border, although it, like the black vulture, is expanding its range to the north. Breeding vultures make no pretense of a nest – their one or two eggs are laid directly on a cliff ledge, the floor of a small cave or the hollow of a rotted tree. The chicks grow slowly, requiring up to 2½ months to fledge. Although the nest site is usually inaccessible, the parents and young have one final defense should an intruder – like a meddlesome bird-watcher – get too close. They regurgitate with an uncanny accuracy, spewing the interloper with whatever noisome carrion they lately fed upon. The trick almost always works.

Turkey vulture: adult

IDENTIFICATION

PLUMAGE: Dark brown body, silvery wing linings, naked red head.

DISTRIBUTION: Southern Canada south to Mexico.

FOOD: Carrion.

NEST: None; cliff ledge, stump, on ground.

EGGS: 2; white with brown spotting

CALIFORNIA CONDOR
GYMNOGYPS CALIFORNIANUS

The largest bird in North America, with a regal wingspan of nearly 10 feet, the California condor ruled the skies of the continent in the post-glacial days of the Pleistocene, when herds of long-horned bison, camels and horses provided plentiful food. But as the climate changed and the great herds disappeared, the condor fell on hard times. Once, it was found as far east as Florida and New York, but by the time the whites settled America, it was restricted to the western mountains and coast.

Even there, the condor was not safe. Shot for its quills or for mindless sport, poisoned by accident when it fed on laced carcasses set out for coyotes, squeezed by agriculture and development into smaller and smaller areas, the condor faded. By 1980 only a handful survived in a remote swath of southern California, and the fight to save the condor from imminent extinction was in full swing.

The outcome of that fight is still very much in question, but the prize is great. The California condor is one of the most awe-inspiring birds – immense black-and-white wings, a fiery orange head and a ruff of glossy black hackles like a feather boa. Sadly, it no longer graces the California skies in the numbers that it did in the past – the last wild condor was trapped in 1987, joining more than two dozen others in captivity, after it was determined that the condor's native habitat had become too "dirty" – awash in pesticides,

heavy metals and other toxins that were quickly killing the species.

The recovery plan hinges on captive breeding, and the eventual release of captive-bred condors into the wild. The process will be slow, because condors do not breed until they are several years old, and even then lay only one egg every other year. Still a major hurdle was overcome in 1989, when the first condors conceived in captivity were born. Meanwhile, Andean condors, a related South American species, were released in former condor habitat, so that when young California condors are finally returned to the wild, there will be experienced adults around to guide the newcomers to roosting and feeding locations. Also under consideration is a plan to release condors in other areas, like the Grand Canyon, where they once occurred, and where the environment is much cleaner.

IDENTIFICATION

PLUMAGE: Black body with white underwing patches, orange head on adult.

DISTRIBUTION: Extinct in wild; formerly southern California.

FOOD: Carrion.

NEST: None; on cliff ledges and caves in remote areas.

EGGS: 1; bluish-white.

California condor: adult

OSPREY

PANDION HALIAETUS

The osprey hunts like no other bird of prey. Hovering high above a shallow lake or pond, the osprey pumps its long wings rhythmically, holding itself stationary for a few moments. Seeing nothing, it peels off, taking up another post, then another. Finally, the osprey's sharp eyes detect a movement below, and it drops.

Unlike the bald eagle, which snatches fish from the surface after a long, shallow dive, the osprey plunges straight down. At the last second it throws back its wings and reaches out with its long legs, talons extended fully. Then it disappears beneath the water in an explosion of spray, surfacing a few seconds later. With sodden, laboring wingbeats it drags itself into the air – often with a fish clutched firmly in its feet.

Fish are virtually all an osprey eats. Its feathers are oily, compact and somewhat water repellent, and the soles of its feet are covered with small spicules that give it a nonslip grip; the outer toe is reversible, forming with the other three an X of claws, also for better holding power. Often called a fish eagle, the osprey is large, with a wingspan of about five feet,

IDENTIFICATION

PLUMAGE: White below, brown above; dark eyestripe and "wrist patches" on wings.

DISTRIBUTION: Coastal; inland through north to Alaska, south to Colorado, New Mexico.

FOOD: Fish, caught by diving.

NEST: Large stick platform built in trees, manmade structures.

EGGS: 2–4; white heavily splotched with brown.

and a crooked-wing flight profile that makes it easy to identify even over long distances. The plumage is brown above and white below, with distinct, dark "elbow" patches on the underwing. Immatures are speckled with white above, and the sexes are similar, except for a faint necklace of flecks on the female's chest.

The osprey's position at the end of a long aquatic food chain got it into trouble in the 1960s and '70s, when concentrations fo DDT and other chlorinated hydrocarbon pesticides in the fish they ate began to poison them out of existence. Thin eggshells and low fertility were the major symptoms, and osprey numbers plummeted, especially on the East Coast where they had been common. Fortunately, stiffer pesticide regulations have removed some of the threat, and ospreys are returning to their former haunts, sometimes aided by reintroduction projects like the one in Pennsylvania; osprey chicks from the healthy Chesapeake Bay population were raised on towers in the Pocono Mountains, then released. Four or five years later, after reaching maturity, some of the released birds returned to nest, the first time the species had bred in the state in decades.

Ospreys are among the most adaptable of raptors when it comes to getting along with humans. In coastal communities, it was once common to erect nest platforms – a wagon wheel at the end of a tall pole – in one's backyard, a practice that is again popular since the osprey's recovery started. They will build their large, bulky stick nest on the tops of harbour buoys, in the masts of wrecked ships and on high-tension wires, as well as such natural locations as trees, cliffs

and, if nothing else is available, on the ground in saltmarshes. The family may number as high as five or six, requiring up to a dozen pounds of fish per day. Because the osprey feeds mostly on small rough fish like suckers, young carp and sunfish, that means plenty of fishing for the harried parents.

Osprey: adult

AMERICAN SWALLOW-TAILED KITE
ELANOIDES FORFICATUS

The swallow-tailed kite was once far more common in the eastern U.S., and that it is no longer found in much of its former range is a tragedy indeed, for this is one of the most elegant raptors in the world, with its white body, black wings and deeply forked tail.

A tropical species that reaches its northern limits in the South, the swallow-tailed kite is a locally common breeding bird in South Carolina, Florida and the Gulf states, although even here it seems to be fighting a losing battle. Once, it was found as far north as Minnesota, and a few overshoot their breeding grounds each spring to show up in such far-flung spots as New Jersey and Colorado, setting off an understandable wave of excitement among bird-lovers.

No other North American raptor looks like a swallow-tailed kite, or flies with such perfect ease and grace. The largest of the four kites, the swallow-tailed is almost as big as an osprey – a shock to many seeing the bird for the first time, who were somehow expecting a dainty bird in keeping with its delicate lines. Large insects, amphibians, snakes, lizards and small birds form its diet, and food is often consumed on the wing. This is a bird that does as much as possible on the wing, even drinking, as it swoops low over the water and skims its beak along the surface for a sip, or catches water on its wing for a mid-air bath. Alone among raptors, it is said to have been observed feeding on ripe fruit, although by no means do all ornithologists accept that contention.

The nest is laboriously built with small twigs, snapped off in the adults' feet, then lined with Spanish moss. The favoured site is the top of a hill, thin pine tree or in a mangrove, and the nest-building – which may expand on the remains of the previous year's nest – is usually finished by mid-March, when the two

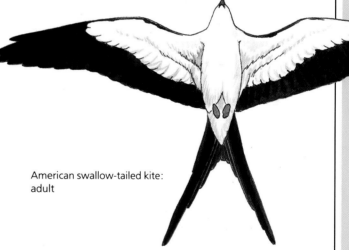

American swallow-tailed kite:
adult

or three eggs are laid. The chicks spend about five weeks in the nest before fledging.

As a bird that relies on forested swamps and marshland for its nesting and hunting, the swallow-tailed kite has two strikes against it. Such habitats have long been drained or timbered, destroying the areas kites – and many other wetland species – need to survive. Illegal shooting and pesticide use, especially on the kite's wintering grounds, aggravate the problem, and only time will tell if this beautiful bird will continue its unfortunate decline.

IDENTIFICATION

PLUMAGE: White body; black wings and long, forked tail.

DISTRIBUTION: Southeast; declining.

FOOD: Insects, small animals.

NEST: Stick and twigs, built very high in trees.

EGGS: 2; white splotched with brown.

BLACK-SHOULDERED KITE
ELANUS CAERULEUS

What's in a name? For years, this bird was known as the white-tailed kite, *Elanus leucurus*. As the only North American kite with a light tail, the common name fitted, but ornithologists eventually decided that, despite difference in wing and tail structure, this was the same species found in Eurasia and Africa, and known as the black-shouldered kite, *Elanus caeruleus*. Because the Eurasian form was named first – and because the first name given a species usually is given priority by scientists – the name of the North American kite was changed to conform.

By any name, the black-shouldered kite is an attractive bird. In flight, from below, one has the overall impression of whiteness, with some darkening toward the primaries and a black patch at the end of each wing. Perched, the black shoulder patches stand out clearly from the pale gray wings and back feathers. The wingspan is about 3½ feet, and the long tail, unlike the swallow-tailed kite's, is squared-off at the tip. Even at a distance too great for field marks, it is possible to identify a black-shouldered kite by its hunting behaviour, for it hovers energetically like a large, white kestrel.

IDENTIFICATION

PLUMAGE: Adult: white undersides, gray back and wings, black shoulder patch. Juvenile: head, breast streaked with russet.

DISTRIBUTION: Texas Gulf coast, California.

FOOD: Small mammals, insects.

NEST: Large twig cup built in treetops.

EGGS: 4–5; white with brown splotches.

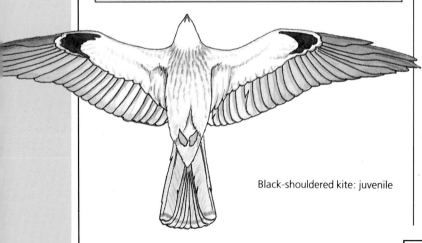
Black-shouldered kite: juvenile

In an era when many raptors are declining because of environmental changes, it is encouraging to watch the black-shouldered kite continue a strong rebound from near-extirpation over much of its range. Illegal shooting almost eliminated the bird in Texas, and seriously reduced its numbers in California, but protection – and the conversion of land to agriculture, which produces plenty of small rodents and insects – have brought on a renaissance. Today, the black-shouldered kite continues to increase in California, where it is again common in open lowlands and along unmowed highway easements, as well as in Texas, and it appears to be recolonizing some of its former range along the Gulf coast.

The black-shouldered's breeding biology is similar to the other common kites. The twig nest is built by both sexes in the uppermost brances of a deciduous tree; the pair usually picks a spot near a wetland or in a riparian habitat along a stream, and in good locations may nest in loose colonies. The clutch is large for a kite, usually four or five eggs – all the more remarkable considering that the male does all the hunting for the chicks, his mate and himself through the whole nesting period. Black-shouldered kites feed heavily on mice, voles, rats and gophers, as well as reptiles and amphibians and insects – food that is abundant in the farm areas and grasslands they generally hunt.

SNAIL KITE
ROSTRHAMUS SOCIABILIS

For want of a snail, a hawk was almost lost – the snail (or Everglades) kite, a tropical species that was one of the first birds to be added to the U.S. endangered species list.

The most specialized of all North American raptors, the snail kite only eats snails of the genus *Pomacea*, which in southern Florida means the apple snail, a large, greenish mollusc that lives in among flooded marsh grass. The snail kite was once common over most of Florida, but massive drainage and diversion of wetlands has reduced its habitat substantially. That, coupled with once-rampant illegal shooting, brought the kite population down to less than 20 birds by the early 1960s.

Protection helped stop the slide, and intensive management for apple snails – as well as the erection of baskets to hold kites' flimsy nests of sticks – has set the stage for a recovery. Today there may be as many as 700 snail kites in the wetland region from Lake Okeechobee south towards the Everglades, although their future is still tied to the wise use of water and preservation of vital funds.

The snail kite is one of the few raptors that are sexually dimorphic in color – that is, the sexes are colored differently. A male is slate-gray, with a white tail that carries a wide black terminal band; his legs and beak are reddish-orange. The female is russet-brown, heavily streaked below with buff, and has a distinct facial pattern that combines a buff background with a dark eyestripe and nape; she, too, has a black-banded tail.

In flight, both sexes show a broad, round-wing silhouette, with a long, squared tail and a habit of dropping to the water's surface to hover as they pluck snails.

Long legs and toes help the kite catch snails, but the bird's most notable adaptation to its lifestyle is its bill, which is long, thin and sharply curved. Once a meal has been caught, the kite grips the snail in one foot and slides its beak between the shell and the operculum, the hard plate that the snail uses to close itself in when danger threatens. The beak then snips the muscle that holds the operculum shut, and the kite pulls the snail out and swallows it. As snails go, the apple snail is fairly large, but a kite must still eat upwards of three dozen a day to survive. In drought, when snail populations are low, the kites are forced to wander beyond their normal range to find suitable wetlands. In these dry years breeding may not take place at all, and the kites may gather in flocks where food can be found. This habit of flocking, as well as a tendency to nest in small colonies, accounts in part for the scientific name, *Rostrhamus sociabilis* (*Rostrhamus* means "hook-billed".)

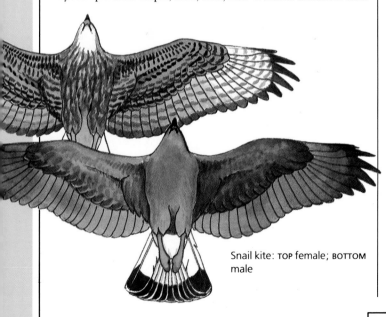

Snail kite: TOP female; BOTTOM male

IDENTIFICATION

PLUMAGE: Male: dark gray, white tail with wide black band. Female: dark brown, similar tail pattern.

DISTRIBUTION: Endangered; southcentral Florida.

FOOD: Apple snails.

NEST: Stick and weed platform in low shrub.

EGGS: 3–4; white, heavily marked with brown.

MISSISSIPPI KITE
ICTINIA MISSISSIPPIENSIS

Perhaps there is such a thing as being *too* successful – at least from an average person's perspective. The Mississippi kite is a prime example. The planting of thousands of wooded shelter belts across the southern Plains has created a paradise for this crow-sized raptor, which is dramatically increasing its numbers and range. All well and good, but the Mississippi kite likes to nest in places like small towns, city parks and, especially, golf courses – they defend their nests with determined ferocity. A golfer preparing to putt, or a housewife hanging out the laundry, are liable to find themselves the target of a blistering aerial attack.

Never mind that the attacking birds rarely strike – for most people, having a hawk with blood-red eyes coming diving out of the clouds is an unnerving experience, particularly if the attacker is joined by a dozen or more other kites, for this species routinely gangs up on what they consider intruders in their territory.

Although the Mississippi kite is found over much of the Southeast, it is most common on the southern Great Plains, from Kansas and Texas through Oklahoma, where oak groves and treebelts dot the prairie. At one time it seems likely that the kite was restricted to natural woodlands along river systems, but man's propensity for planting trees opened up vast new areas, for the Mississippi kite likes to hunt open country but nest in small groves. Today, it is the most common raptor in its Plains habitat – and becoming even more so.

The adults are strikingly colored: dark gray above, lighter gray below, with dark primaries contrasting with silvery secondaries. Black feathers rim the red eyes, giving the bird the appearance of deep-set

sockets. Its long, tapered wings and tail, as well as its command of the air, are very much like a peregrine falcon's and have fooled more than one hawk-watcher. Immature birds are brown above and heavily streaked below, with banded tails.

The Mississippi kite is a confirmed insect-eater, snatching dragonflies from the air and grasshoppers, cicadas and other large bugs from the ground; males also take a few rodents, reptiles, frogs and nestling birds.

As defensive as kites may be toward humans, they are often gregarious among others of their own species, even during the breeding season. One researcher in Kansas observed more than 100 kites using a 50-acre woodlot in a state park that was surrounded by grassland and fields, and smaller colonies are common.

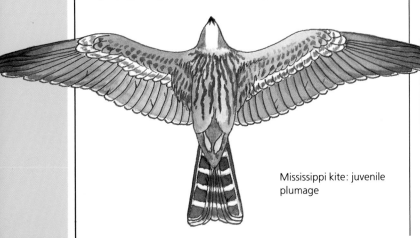

Mississippi kite: juvenile plumage

IDENTIFICATION

PLUMAGE: Adult: gray below, dark gray above with black primaries and squared tail. Juvenile: heavily streaked with brown.

DISTRIBUTION: Southeast and southern Plains.

FOOD: Insects, some small mammals.

NEST: Stick and twig platform in tall trees, often in loose colonies.

EGGS: 1–3; white.

BALD EAGLE
HALIAEETUS LEUCOCEPHALUS

John James Audubon can be forgiven for the mistake. In 1814, while travelling on the Mississippi River between Missouri and Illinois, he spotted a huge, all-brown eagle, which he declared to be a new species. "The Bird of Washington," or the Washington sea-eagle. While Audubon must have been aware that immature bald eagles don't achieve their white head until they are several years old, the bird's very large size apparently convinced him that this was an entirely different species. He simply didn't know that the northern bald eagles that breed in the Great Lakes region and Canada are considerably bigger than those he was used to seeing; there is also the very good chance that the bird was a female, for female eagles – like most raptors – are noticeably larger than males.

Anyone who has watched an eagle soar can relate to Audubons excitement, however. Bald eagles have a mystique about them that rivets one's attention – the white head and tail shimmering in the sun, the wings and body so dark brown that they look black, the massive yellow beak and piercing eye. Ben Franklin may (jokingly) have suggested the wild turkey as the U.S. national symbol, but few today would argue that the eagle fills that role superbly.

One would think that a bird so big and well-known would be easy to identify, but that is not always the case. An adult in good light is unmistakable, although ospreys, which have lots of white on the head, and turkey vultures (which are, after all, "bald") are frequently mistaken for bald eagles. The problem birds are the brown immature eagles. Only in the last 10 years have birders sorted out the confusing plumage changes that bald eagles go through in the four years it takes to attain adult color. Soon after leaving the nest, the fledglings – which are by then as large as their parents – are chocolate brown above and below, with whitish wing linings underneath. By the next spring they molt into the "white-belly" plumage, which they carry for two years; there is a great deal of white mottling on the belly, back, wing linings and tail. By age three, the young eagles are developing

Bald eagle: 2-year-old

the white head and tail of an adult, and gradually lose the light mottling elsewhere.

At any point in these immature stages, a young bald eagle is easy to mistake for a golden eagle. Both are large birds, with wingspans approaching seven or eight feet. But while the golden eagle has a long tail and a fairly short head, the bald eagle's oversized beak gives the impression of a head almost as long as the tail. The wings are plank-shaped, with a straight trailing edge (pinched inward in golden eagles) and a flat soaring profile (which in goldens shows a slight dihedral.)

These are somewhat brighter days for bald eagles. In the 1950s and '60s, dangerous pesticides like DDT, habitat loss, illegal shooting and water pollution had eliminated them from much of the Lower 48. Many of the eagles that remained were so loaded with toxins that they could not lay fertile eggs, or incubate their clutch without crushing the unnaturally thin eggshells. The growing environmental movement, with its "Ban DDT" slogans and beefed-up protection for eagles, came just in time. Today bald eagles, while still an endangered or threatened species in most of their range, are increasing at a slow but steady pace. Helping the natural growth, states like New York and Massachusetts have used hacking techniques developed for peregrine falcons to return bald eagle chicks to regions where they were eliminated.

The bald eagle is not out of the woods, however. Because it lives and fishes in the same watery areas that people enjoy for recreation, there is growing concern that human disturbance may send the bald eagle on yet another downward spiral. Nor are pesticide dangers a thing of the past; between 1985 and 1989, 23 bald eagles in the Chesapeake Bay region were poisoned with carbofuran, a controversial chemical used mostly on cornfields.

Across much of Canada and Alaska, bald eagles have fared better, living in largely undisturbed wilderness. The bald eagle is a fish-eater, catching its prey near the surface or feeding on dead fish washed to shore; it also has a taste for carrion, and will capture sick or crippled waterfowl when it can. It has a reputation for piracy, stealing fish from smaller birds like osprey and crows, although this behaviour is not as common as once thought. Eagles will congregate by the hundreds along rivers that have heavy salmon runs. On the Chilkat River on southeast Alaska, up to 4,000 bald eagles gather each November to feast on the dead and dying salmon – truly a sight to behold.

IDENTIFICATION

PLUMAGE: Adult: unmistakable white head and tail, dark body. Immature: brown overall, with varying amounts of white on body and wing linings.

DISTRIBUTION: Breeds coastally, interior Canada, Great Lakes and West. Also winters in much of mid-continent.

FOOD: Fish, carrion, some birds and mammals.

NEST: Large, bulky mass of sticks high in a tree.

EGGS: 2; white.

NORTHERN HARRIER
CIRCUS CYANEUS

The harrier is a hawk apart. Its face, with eyes set within a circular ruff of feathers, is quite owlish. It spends much of its time near or on the ground and builds its nest there, rather than in the branches of a tree or on a cliff. Even its hunting flight is unhawklike – a slow, buoyant meander on raised wings, weaving only a few yards above the ground.

Known for years as the marsh hawk, the harrier is most often found in wetlands and grassy habitats. Although it takes some songbirds, invertebrates, reptiles and amphibians, the vast majority of its diet is made up of small rodents, especially meadow voles, those short-tailed "field mice" that are among the most common of mammals.

Like many animals, voles are subject to boom-and-bust population cycles, which run on a roughly four-year schedule. At the low point in the cycle, harriers may not breed at all, and those that do will have small clutches of eggs. But when the cycle peaks, and voles are present in unbelievable numbers, the harriers make up for lost time by producing batches of up to nine or 10 chicks, and by practicing polygyny to insure that every mature female possible has mated.

Harriers are dimorphic in size and color; the smaller adult males are pale gray, with black wingtips, while the bigger females are brown above and streaked with brown below. Both sexes have a large white rump patch which, along with its turkey vulture-like flight, makes them easy to identify. Immature birds (often seen at fall hawk-watches) are similar to adult females, but have a wash of deep cinnamon over the breast and belly.

The female harrier takes primary responsibility for nest-building, selecting a hummock in marshy ground near low shrubs, then building a platform of sticks, twigs and weeds. Unlike many hawks, harriers do not

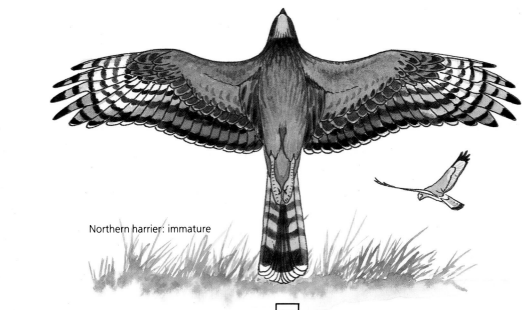

Northern harrier: immature

mate for life, or even for the long-term. Males attract a mate by performing an intricate "sky dance" that involves rolls, loops and a ritual passing of food from the male to the female. If the male takes only one mate he will help hunt for the chicks, but a polygynous male will leave subsequent mates to supply their own young with food – a reason why the nests of polygamous harriers are less successful than monogamous harriers.

IDENTIFICATION

PLUMAGE: Male: light below, gray above with black wingtips. Female and juvenile: brown or rusty. All show white rump patch.

DISTRIBUTION: Breeds or winters over most of continent near grasslands or marshes.

FOOD: Small mammals, some birds, reptiles, amphibians.

EGGS: 4–6; white with faint brownish markings.

SHARP-SHINNED HAWK
ACCIPITER STRIATUS

Small size never stopped a sharp-shinned hawk. This smallest of the accipiters, or forest hawks, may be little larger than a blue jay, but it will not hesitate to tackle prey much bigger than itself. Songbirds are a sharp-shinned's usual diet, but pigeons, rabbits and even chickens have fallen to its devil-may-care attacks.

The old country name for the sharp-shinned, "blue darter," sums up its coloration and behaviour. Adults are blue-gray above, with russet barring on the breast and dark bands on the tail. Immature birds are brown above, with brown streaking below and assorted white spots on the back. Actually, the eye is the best indicator of age; a first-year bird has a yellow iris, which darkens through orange to the bright red hue of an adult, at about three years of age. Many sharp-shinneds in adult plumage will still lack the bright red eye for a year.

As with all accipiters, the sharp-shinned has a long, narrow tail and rounded, comparatively short wings that present an easily reconizable flight silhouette. Just as distinctive are the "sharpie's" rapid-fire wingbeats, interspersed with short glides, although they will soar in a thermal like a buteo. As easy as it is to differentiate sharp-shinneds from most other hawks, even the experts can have trouble telling this bird from the Cooper's hawk, a slightly larger accipiter that is almost identical in appearance. Look for the sharp-shinned's squared (rather than rounded) tail, fairly small head and faster wingbeats.

Size is little help, because accipiters display the greatest degree of sexual size difference in raptors. Female sharp-shinned hawks may be half again as heavy as their mates – and almost the same size as a small male Cooper's hawk. In the natural world, males are usually the bigger of the two sexes, so why is that standard reversed in many raptors? There are several theories, including that the female needs more body mass to produce eggs, or to shield her from attacks by her mate. Most likely, though, the different sizes allow a pair to take a wider variety of food – the small male hunting agile songbirds, the bigger female taking heavier, stronger creatures.

Sharpies breed in mixed forests over the northern half of the continent, down the Appalachians and over much of the West; in winter they retreat from their northernmost territory into the U.S. They are not uncommon at backyard birdfeeders – although not for sunflower seed. Attracted by unnatural concentrations of songbirds, a sharp-shinned may spend the winter working a circuit of feeders, picking off the slow and weak from the flocks – and driving bird-loving humans, who don't realize that this is how nature works, to absolute distraction.

IDENTIFICATION

PLUMAGE: Adult: blue-gray upperparts, rusty-barred breast. Immatures: brown upperparts, brown-streaked breast.

DISTRIBUTION: Breeds Appalachians, New England, West and Canada. Winters over most of U.S.

FOOD: Primarily small birds, some mammals.

NEST: Stick platform, usually in conifer in mixed woodlands.

EGGS: 3–4; white with bright brown wreathing.

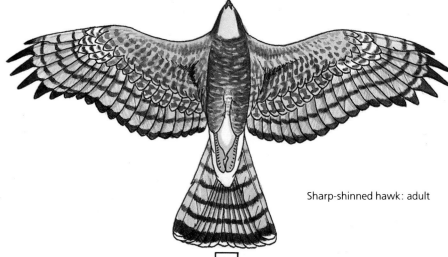

Sharp-shinned hawk: adult

COOPER'S HAWK
ACCIPITER COOPERII

A larger version of the sharp-shinned hawk, the Cooper's hawk is more southerly in its breeding range, but far less common – and there is concern that it may be declining even further, for reasons not fully understood.

Like the sharp-shinned, the immature Cooper's carries brown-streaked plumage for its first year, then gradually molts into the blue-and-russet adult coloration. The tail is somewhat longer, and the adult has a buffy neck nape that contrasts with a dark gray crown – a field mark absent in the sharp-shinned. Size is highly variable; a small male Cooper's may be 14 or 15 inches long, with a wingspan of about 28 inches, while a big female may be 20 inches long, with a nearly three-foot wingspan.

In the days when every farm had a flock of free-roaming chickens, this species was the hated "chicken hawk," occasionally grabbing a pullet before disappearing into the safety of the woods again. Unfortunately, the farmer would rarely see the culprit, so the red-tailed hawk circling the fields for rodents usually got the blame – and the buckshot. Today, chickens are raised in barns and Cooper's hawks (which are, like all raptors, fully protected) rarely get into trouble with humans. They will patrol birdfeeders in winter, and pigeon fanciers know that a Cooper's hawk can wreak havoc on their flocks, but by and large the friction between man and hawk is a thing of the past.

Cooper's hawk: LEFT immature plumage; CENTER adult in flight; RIGHT adult plumage

Deciduous woods are the preferred habitat for Cooper's hawks, although, like many hawks, they may seek out a tall conifer to hold their nest. The flat platform of sticks is built primarily by the female, who as a finishing touch lines it with large chips of bark. Four or five eggs are the norm, with incubation taking just over a month. The chicks are born alert, with open eyes and a thick coat of white natal down – and with ceaselessly hungry stomachs. The parents hunt hard to keep them fed, but oddly, they rarely hunt in the vicinity of the nest. Medium-sized songbirds make up most of the diet – woodpeckers, grackles, starlings, robins, jays, doves and the like; if they are abundant, small mammals like chipmunks, red squirrels, mice and rats are also taken. The kill comes after a short, head-long chase through dense cover, where the Cooper's long tail allows it to maneuver with uncanny ease. This is a bird that does not give up easily – it has been seen chasing prey into thickets on foot, and an animal may be dunked into a handy creek and drowned.

IDENTIFICATION

PLUMAGE: Same as sharp-shinned hawk.

DISTRIBUTION: Uncommon over most of U.S. and southern Canada.

FOOD: Primarily birds, some small mammals.

NEST: Large stick platform, lined with chips of bark.

EGGS: 4–5; off-white.

GOSHAWK
ACCIPITER GENTILIS

As beautiful and mysterious as the trackless northern forests where it is most common, a goshawk is a bird that must be sought out. Few pass the fall hawk-watches, so a day when two or three of these big, gray birds are sighted is a day to be treasured in memory.

The goshawk is the biggest and rarest of the accipiters. Larger than a crow, with a thick body and wide tail, in flight it resembles a buteo more than a sharp-shinned or a Cooper's hawk. The wingbeats are slow and deep – everything about this bird bespeaks power.

Coniferous forests in Canada, the northern states and the western mountains are home for the goshawk, which is far less tolerant of human intrusion than the other two accipiters. In many respects this is a wilderness bird, although the regeneration of mature forests in the Appalachians has brought increased reports of breeding goshawks from more southerly locations like Pennsylvania.

Immature goshawks have the standard accipiter brown back and streaked undersides. The adult, however, is far different. The back and wings are a rich gray with a touch of blue, while the undersides are finely barred with gray, giving a silvery appearance at any distance. The gray tail is crossed by four heavy,

IDENTIFICATION

PLUMAGE: Adult: gray above, pale gray below, white eyestripe. Immature: brown above, breast white with brown streaks.

DISTRIBUTION: Boreal forests across Canada, Western mountains; rare in Appalachians.

FOOD: Large birds, hares, squirrels, crows.

NEST: Large, flat stick structure lined with bark, built high in tree.

EGGS: 2–4; unmarked, off-white.

dark bands, and a white eyestripe cuts through the dark head.

The goshawk is so big and strong it comes as no surprise that it takes fairly large prey. In the north woods, snowshoe hares, spruce and ruffed grouse, cottontail rabbits and large songbirds are most frequently eaten; in mixed forests to the south of its range, crows and red squirrels were found to be of primary importance. Because of their fancied toll on game animals, goshawks were subjected to bounties for many years. This archaic practice is a thing of the past, thankfully, and biologists now realize that predators like goshawks have no significant impact on prey populations. Of far more importance – to hawk and prey alike – is preservation of quality habitat.

A goshawk's nest is usually high in a coniferous or deciduous tree, a bulky cup of twigs and sticks placed in a crotch of the tree. The parents – especially the female – are ferocious defenders, and biologists who must climb to the nest to band the chicks routinely wear heavy coats and helmets to ward off the frenzied attacks.

Every 10 years or so, northern goshawks stage "invasions" into the south, presumably in response to a low point in the population cycle of their prey. Such irruptions (as they are correctly known) are exciting times for birders, who may find this most boreal of birds as far south as the Gulf of Mexico.

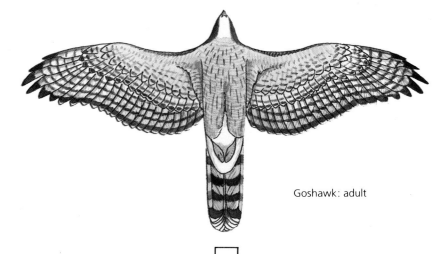

Goshawk: adult

COMMON BLACK-HAWK
BUTEOGALLUS ANTHRACINUS

The common black-hawk is one of five buteos that are largely tropical in their distribution, and only enter the U.S. in the extreme Southwest.

Rare and local, this is a bird of riparian habitat, that is, woodlands and thickets that grow along streams or rivers. In the West such habitat is under pressure from increasing human use, for recreation, cattle-ranching and housing, and the wildlife that depends upon it – like the black-hawk – is caught in the squeeze.

During the breeding season, small numbers of black-hawks can be found in southern Arizona, south-western New Mexico and the Big Bend region of Texas. They rarely stray from water, because they feed largely on crayfish, frogs, fish, crabs, snakes and lizards. Little is known about its breeding biology; the nests that have been found were in tall trees such as pines and cypress, and the usual number of eggs seems to be one or two.

In flight, it is easy to mistake a black-hawk for a black vulture, since both species have wide, dark wings and very short tails. The black-hawk's tail, however, is banded with three black-and-white bars, and it lacks the black vulture's prominent white wing patches, although it does show some white at the base of the primaries. Immatures are dark brown above, with a buff breast heavily streaked in brown and a noticeable light eye stripe; there is also a dark malar stripe coming down off each corner of the mouth. The legs at any age are rather long, a feature most apparent when the bird is perched.

Black-hawks hunt by perching over water, watching patiently for prey to show itself below, by walking along banks and mudbars, hoping to surprise a crab away from its burrow, or find a fish caught in shallow water.

IDENTIFICATION

PLUMAGE: Adult: black overall, with white tail band and white patches under wings. Juvenile: brown, heavily streaked, with thin tail bands.

DISTRIBUTION: Southern Arizona, New Mexico, Big Bend region of Texas.

FOOD: Crayfish, frogs, snakes, lizards, fish.

NEST: Stick structure lined with green leaves, in tree near water.

EGGS: 1–2; white with fine brown spotting.

Common black-hawk: adult

HARRIS' HAWK
PARABUTEO UNICINCTUS

An inhabitant of semiarid brushland and dry forests in Texas, New Mexico and Arizona, the Harris' hawk is notable not just for its physical beauty – this is one of the prettiest buteos – but also for its unusual life history, which scientists are just beginning to unravel.

In the hot, dry lands where this large hawk lives, desert cottontails and jackrabbits are among the most common mammals. But a rabbit is swift and agile, hard work for any hawk to chase and capture. Harris' hawks have solved this problem with an approach rarely seen in raptors – cooperative hunting involving more than two birds. A team of researchers in New Mexico discovered that Harris' hawks will hunt in groups of up to a half-dozen birds, surrounding cover where rabbits might be hiding. One hawk rushes in to flush the rabbit, which bolts, leaving its attacker behind. Ordinarily this gambit would work, but when it makes its break, the rabbit finds itself set upon by the other hawks. Once the kill is made, the hunters share the meal among themselves – another very unusual behaviour for a hawk. Other common prey items include birds, reptiles and large insects.

The oddities don't end there. Many Harris' hawk pairs have "nest helpers," unmated birds that assist in rearing the chicks. This was once thought to be a form of polyandry, but closer study revealed that the helpers do not mate with the reproducing female. Although group nests experience a higher rate of nest failure than nests cared for by pairs, the nestlings from group nests grew to a larger size, suggesting that the young in such situations are better fed.

Roughly the size of a red-tailed hawk, the Harris' hawk has a proportionately longer tail and long legs. The adult plumage is a handsome combination of chocolate brown, with reddish shoulders, underwing linings and thighs; the tail is black, with a broad white base. The immature has a streaked breast, and when seen from below, the primaries are much lighter than in the adult.

Nesting takes place in cactus or small trees like mesquite and soapberry. The nest itself is fairly large, with a lining of soft grass, leaves or bark. Two or three eggs make up the average clutch, and second or even third broods have been recorded in Arizona.

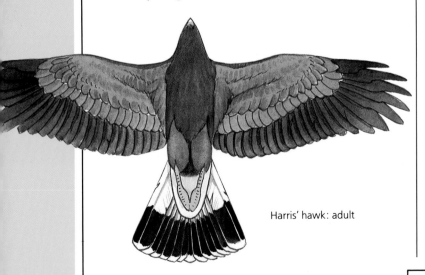

Harris' hawk: adult

IDENTIFICATION

PLUMAGE: Adult: chocolate-brown body with chestnut wing linings, shoulder patches, thighs; white tail with wide black band. Immature: paler, streaked breast.

DISTRIBUTION: West Texas, southeast New Mexico, southern Arizona.

FOOD: Rabbits, jackrabbits, birds, reptiles.

NEST: Stick platform in low tree, lined with green leaves.

EGGS: 2–3; white.

GRAY HAWK
BUTEO NITIDUS

The gray hawk is a buteo that thinks it's an accipiter – or at least it seems that way, judging from how this Mexican border species flies.

Flashy and quick, using rapid wingbeats and short glides, the gray hawk hunts mostly for lizards, which it snatches as they scurry for cover; small birds, snakes, rodents, insects and even fish are also taken, with the hawk hunting from a perch or while soaring.

In size and shape, the gray hawk is quite similar to the broad-winged hawk, a far more common species. The wings are wide and somewhat pointed, the tail a bit longer, in proportion, than in most buteos. The adult is gray – solid above, barred below, with a black-and-white banded tail, a pattern that explains one of its names, the Mexican goshawk. The immature is, like so many young buteos, brown above and streaked below, with a tail of fine brown bars. The wingspan for all ages is a little under three feet.

The gray hawk is a member of the United States' avifauna by the scantest margin. A tropical bird, it barely enters the U.S. as a breeding species in southeastern Arizona, where it is uncommon near running water, and in the lower Rio Grande valley, where a few pairs live year-round.

The small nest is built near the top of a cottonwood or other streamside tree, and lined with green leaves. Many hawks follow this practice of bringing greenery to the nest, and biologists now believe the birds are practicing a natural form of pest control. Cherry leaves, for example, emit a small quantity of cyanide gas as they wilt – not enough to harm the birds, but apparently enough to drive away parasites and insect pests. This behavior is especially apt to occur in hawks that reuse their nests from year to year, or to raise a second brood in the same season.

As with the black-hawk, little is known about the gray hawk's life history. The two eggs are incubated for about 30 days, and the young spend another four or five weeks in the nest. It is known that the male is capable of rearing the young if the female is killed, something not every species of hawk is able to do; in some, like the northern harrier, the male's instinct is to bring whole food to the nest, but not to tear into small pieces and present it to the chicks. If the babies are still too small to handle whole prey, they will die of starvation surrounded by food.

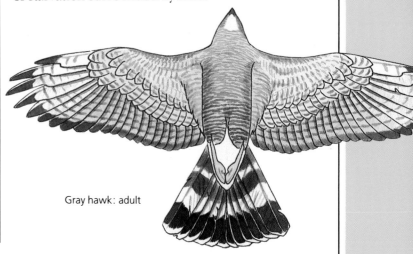

Gray hawk: adult

IDENTIFICATION

PLUMAGE: Adult: gray upperparts, fine gray barring on breast, banded tail. Immature: brown above, brown breast streaking.

DISTRIBUTION: Mexican border.

FOOD: Lizards, snakes, small birds, small mammals.

NEST: Small twig bowl concealed in high treetop.

EGGS: 2–3; white.

BROAD-WINGED HAWK
BUTEO PLATYPTERUS

Like the red-shouldered, the broad-winged hawk is a bird of mature eastern and northern forests, living among trees that have grown tall enough to close off the canopy and shade the ground.

The broad-winged is a small raptor, the most diminutive of the buteos, only 16 inches long with a wingspan of about 34 or 35 inches. It is a chunky hawk both at rest and in flight; in the air, the wings are wide and pointed, the tail very broad and the head small. An adult broad-winged will have a brown back and head, chestnut barred breast and a very boldly banded tail of black and white. First-year birds are confusingly similar to red-shouldered hawks, with plenty of brown streaking and a brown-banded tail.

Broad-wingeds are common over most of the East, and in a band from Quebec to Alberta in Canada, wherever diciduous and mixed forests are found. Although they are often seen soaring high over the canopy, most of their hunting is done quietly from low perches. Broad-wingeds are nonselective in their prey, as long as it is fairly small – mice and voles, shrews, snakes, frogs, lizards, young birds, crayfish and large insects. Clearings like power-line corridors are favoured hunting locations, and broad-wingeds are frequently seen perched along the edge of interstates that cut through hardwood forests. They are exceptionally tame, and when flushed may only fly a short distance before landing again; this may be repeated a dozen or more times before the hawk finally flaps away into the woods, complaining with a high, descending whistle as it goes.

Soon after the hawks return in the spring, nesting territories are set up, and a new nest is built. A hardwood tree is the usual site, hidden away from disturbance (although broad-wingeds will occasionally nest in a wooded subdivision, or along a busy road). Two chicks are average, but as many as four may be raised in an exceptional year.

The fall broad-winged hawk migration is the high point of autumn for many Eastern birders. The flight begins in early September, when cold fronts from Canada trigger the urge to head south. Broad-wingeds follow the mountain ridge systems down New England and along the Appalachians, although they are not tied to them as rigidly as are other hawks, and a day when good thermals beckon in the valleys, the flight will move south in a broad front, rather than concentrating along a mountain flyway.

The numbers can be astounding. Broad-wingeds regularly fly in large flocks (known as kettles,) and on a good day the sky is filled with swirling masses of birds. At Hawk Mountain Sanctuary in Pennsylvania, September 14, 1979 is still referred to as "the miracle day," when 21,000 broad-wingeds were tallied. Totals are vastly higher further south, in Texas and especially in Panama, where a continent's worth of broad-wingeds funnel through a tiny area. Their ultimate destination is northern and central South America, where they will pass the winter until it is time to reverse the trip in early spring.

IDENTIFICATION

PLUMAGE: Adult: brown upperparts, chestnut-barred breast, wide black-and-white tail bands. Immature: brown above, brown streaks below, brown-banded tail.

DISTRIBUTION: Eastern woodlands, west through southern Canada.

FOOD: Reptiles, amphibians, small mammals, insects.

NEST: Small stick bowl 50 feet or less from ground.

EGGS: 2–3; white with buffy blotches.

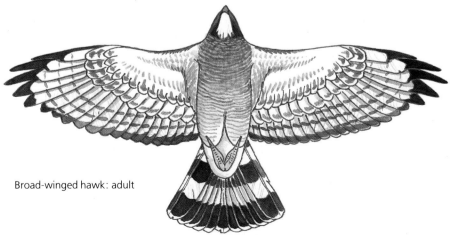

Broad-winged hawk: adult

RED-SHOULDERED HAWK
BUTEO LINEATUS

"Striped broad-winged hawk," is the rough translation of the red-shouldered hawk's Latin name, but that hardly does justice to this beautiful species, which is found in the moist woodlands of the East. An isolated population in California is known there as the red-bellied hawk, a better moniker that draws attention to the lovely orangish barring that covers the breast of the adults.

The coloration of a mature red-shoulder is intricate. Besides the reddish breast and rusty shoulder patches, the wings are finely striped, above and below, with narrow black and white bands. The tail is barred as well in black and white, and the wing linings are orangish. Young birds are brown with breast streaking, and only a hint of russet under the wings. In flight, the red-shouldered hawk has a typical buteo outline, with longish wings and tail – which, combined with its rapid wingbeat, makes it easy to mistake for an accipiter. Immatures, on the other hand, are routinely misidentified as young broad-winged hawks; look for the red-shoulder's more rounded wingtips. All ages have a translucent, crescent-shaped "wing window" at the base of the primaries, especially obvious if the bird is backlit. Be careful with this field mark, though, because other buteos have translucent panels, usually rectangular.

Where maples and hemlocks grow among thick ferns, or swamp waters reflect the forms of baldcypress, watch for red-shouldered hawks. They are birds of stream and river valleys, forested swamps and damp woods, hunting for small mammals, birds, reptiles, amphibians and crayfish. Because they stick to thick cover more than red-tailed hawks, they are not often seen by the casual observer, causing them to be under-reported in many areas, although there has been a very real decline in red-shouldered hawk populations over the years. At the turn of the century they were the most common buteo in New England, but the logging of mature forests, which were replaced by brush, allowed the red-tail to rise to prominence. Pesticide contamination has been another, persistent problem, with eggshell-thinning widely blamed for recent drops in red-shoulder numbers.

The red-shouldered hawk's nest is a large mass of sticks and twigs, built close to the trunk of a high deciduous tree. The hawks will reuse the nest in subsequent years – if they get the chance. Barred owls, which share their moist-woods habitat, have a penchant for taking over red-shouldered hawk nests. Because the owls generally start nesting activities before the hawks, the red-shoulders must start again elsewhere – a clear case of first come, first served.

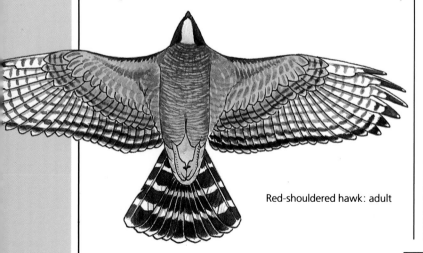

Red-shouldered hawk: adult

IDENTIFICATION

PLUMAGE: Adult: chestnut breast, shoulder patches; fine black barring on wings, tail. Immature: brown above, white breast streaked with brown, brown-barred tail.

DISTRIBUTION: Moist Eastern forests: disjunct population in California.

FOOD: Small mammals, reptiles, amphibians, crayfish, some birds.

NEST: Bulky stick, twig nest lined with bark, leaves.

EGGS: 2–3; pale or buff, flecked with brown.

SHORT-TAILED HAWK
BUTEO BRACHYURUS

Another tropical species that reaches its extreme northern limit in the U.S., the short-tailed hawk is a rare bird of south Florida.

With most birds, there is a single plumage pattern each for the immature and adult stages, but a few birds exhibit color phases, or morphs. A phase has nothing to do with sex or age, and different phases may occur in the same nest of babies. The short-tailed hawk is one of several North American raptors that have colors phases – a light phase and a dark phase, in this case. In Florida, dark birds are somewhat more common. A dark phase adult is solid, brownish-black above and below, with gray, barred wing linings and a finely banded tail. The light phase is so completely different that it was, for years, considered a separate species; the back and wings are brown, the undersides are white, although the tail in this phase, too, is light gray with fine black bands. Dark-phase and light-phase birds will interbreed, but the chicks will be either dark or light – there are no intergrades, as with some raptor morphs.

The short-tailed hawk is a small buteo, not much larger than a broad-winged. It is a bird hunter, somewhat unusual for a buteo, since the group as a whole tends to take mostly rodents and cold-blooded prey. A short-tail on the hunt "kites," holding itself stationary in the wind high above the ground, carefully scanning the savannah or forest below. When a small bird bolts into the open, the hawk drops quickly to the attack.

Details of its life history are sketchy. The large nest is built near the top of a tree, often a baldcypress or mangrove in a swamp, and is adorned with sprigs of green leaves. The breeding season in Florida begins in January, with two eggs most often making up the complete clutch. Almost nothing is known about how long the incubation and nestling period lasts, much less how many more weeks the chicks are reliant on their parents for food.

IDENTIFICATION

PLUMAGE: Light phase: white underparts, brown upperparts, banded tail. Dark phase: all-brown body, banded light primaries and secondaries.

DISTRIBUTION: Central and southern Florida.

FOOD: Primarily birds.

NEST: Twig and leaf nest built in treetop near water.

EGGS: 2–3; white, often spotted with brown.

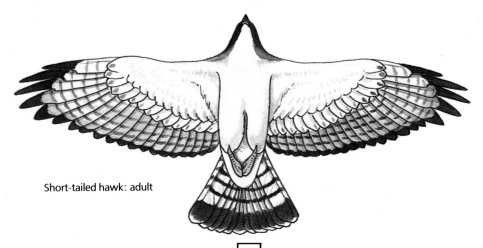

Short-tailed hawk: adult

SWAINSON'S HAWK
BUTEO SWAINSONI

Although the Swainson's hawk is found in open land from central Alaska to the eastern Great Plains, it is a raptor that most people associate with the sagebrush country of the West, where it is a common sight on fenceposts and utility poles, or wheeling in the shimmering heat of midday.

This is a big, tame bird, easily approachable even in areas where it has been needlessly persecuted for generations. As large as a red-tailed hawk, the Swainson's is less powerful and has smaller feet, in keeping with its diet of grasshoppers, crickets, mice and occasional small birds. In a sense, the Swainson's is the Plains counterpart to the woodland broad-wing – a trusting hunter of small animals that travels in large flocks. It is like the broad-winged in another important sense, for the Swainson's hawk is highly migratory, moving to the open pampas of Argentina for the austral summer.

There are two color phases, the light being by far the most common. Light-phase birds are brown on the back and wings, with a brownish hood that merges with a distinct bib unlike any other buteo, and white underparts and wing linings. The dark phase is solid brown, lighter under the tail. Both phases have gray tails with a half-dozen dark bands. Some authorities differentiate a third morph, the rufous phase, in which the body color is a deep chestnut. The easiest way to identify a Swainson's hawk is on the wing. In flight its wings are very long and very pointed, carried in a shallow dihedral. The flight is light and airy, as though the bird did not have to work to stay aloft.

Even in wide-open grasslands, the Swainson's hawk seeks out trees in which to nest, usually picking an isolated tree or windbreak to hold the sloppy, ill-made mass of twigs, thistles and grass stems. Like the mourning dove, which suffers because of its lack of construction skills, many Swainson's hawk nests are lost each year to high winds and bad weather. Perhaps for that reason, roughly half of the nesting hawks take over the abandoned nests of other birds, especially black-billed magpies. The average brood is two chicks, which is normal for most buteos.

Life can be hard for Swainson's hawks. Up to 30 percent of the nests may be lost to weather damage, they are still widely shot despite legal protection, cars kill many that attempt to hunt along highways, and untold thousands succumb to the rigors of a migratory round-trip of 17,000 miles.

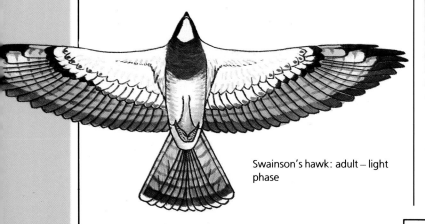
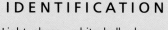

Swainson's hawk: adult – light phase

IDENTIFICATION

PLUMAGE: Light phase: white belly, brown head and chest, banded tail, brown upperparts. Dark phase: dark brown body and wings.

DISTRIBUTION: Western Plains from Texas to southern Yukon.

FOOD: Small mammals and insects.

NEST: Large, messy assemblage of sticks and weeds, built near ground.

EGGS: 2–3; white, sometimes flecked with brown.

WHITE-TAILED HAWK
BUTEO ALBICAUDATUS

The white-tailed hawk is fairly common within its restricted range, on the grassy prairies of the south Texas Gulf coast. It is much more common and widespread to the south, through Mexico, Central and South America – another example of a tropical hawk that reaches its northern terminus in the U.S.

One of the largest North American buteos, the white-tailed hunts for rabbits, small mammals, snakes, lizards and birds, spotted while soaring and caught after a fast dive. Over time, this species has learned that grass fires are a boon for hungry hawks, and a widening smudge of white smoke on the horizon is enough to attract white-tailed hawks from miles around. They gather near the advancing edge of the blaze, snatching panicked animals racing to escape the flames. At such times, large numbers of these beautiful hawks may be feeding together, sharing the bounty of a wildfire.

Adult white-tails have an attractive plumage pattern – gray upperparts with chestnut shoulder patches and back feathers, a white belly scored with fine gray barring, and a white tail with a thick black terminal band and thin gray bars. The first-year birds are very dark gray, with a white blotch in the middle of the

chest that is quite unlike any other young buteo. In flight, the adult's very long, pointed wings and dihedral profile are similar to a Swainson's, but the tail is quite a bit shorter – a fact especially easy to see when the hawk is perched, for the wingtips actually extend beyond the end of the tail.

Many hawks have courtship displays that involve ritualized flight, calls or the passage of prey from male to female. In the white-tailed hawk, the pair may grip talons in midair as they reaffirm their bond. The nest is big, bulky and untidy, bolstered each year with the addition of new material. Nests are built near to the ground in low-growing bushes or short trees, but often on a rise that allows the bird to see over long distances.

White-tailed hawks suffered badly from pesticide contamination of their food, and the resultant eggshell thinning. Just as bad, this bird prefers undisturbed areas of chapparal and grassland, and human activities have steadily whittled away at its habitat.

IDENTIFICATION

PLUMAGE: Gray upperparts, white breast with fine barring, rufous shoulder patches, white tail with dark terminal band.

DISTRIBUTION: Extreme southern Texas.

FOOD: Small mammals, reptiles, amphibians, insects.

NEST: Large, flat platform built in low shrub with good view of surroundings.

EGGS: 2–3; whitish, usually marked with brown.

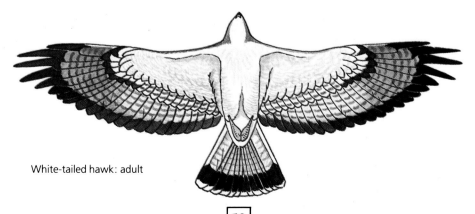

White-tailed hawk: adult

ZONE-TAILED HAWK
BUTEO ALBONOTATUS

Mimicry, so common among reptiles, amphibians, insects and fish, is almost unknown among birds, except for song imitations like those of the mockingbird. Burrowing owls will imitate the buzz of a rattlesnake to frighten predators from their nest holes, but surely the finest example of bird mimicry in North America is the zone-tailed hawk.

A medium-sized buteo of the Southwest, the zone-tailed hawk is dark, sooty gray, with a banded white tail and long, fairly narrow wings. In flight, it carries those wings in a shallow dihedral and rocks back and forth. The color and flight behaviour are a dead-ringer for a turkey vulture.

Turkey vultures, being carrion eaters, present no danger to small animals. By imitating a vulture's appearance, the zone-tailed hawk is presumably able to approach its prey with less chance of frightening it away, and to that end it will often soar with groups of turkey vultures, peeling out of the flock and into a dive when it spots a snake, lizard or mouse.

Mimicry is not a conscious decision on the part of the species; zone-tailed hawks did not "decide" to impersonate vultures. But over time, natural selection exerts pressure in favor of those zone-tailed hawks that look and act like turkey vultures, since they would be more successful at hunting than zone-tailed hawks that do not mimic vultures.

The zone-tailed hawk is uncommon in wooded hills and canyons, especially in riparian habitat near water. Its range overlaps that of the common black-hawk, and the two species can be very confusing in the air; the zone-tailed has much narrower wings, a tail that appears proportionately longer and primary feathers that, like a turkey vulture's, look lighter than the wing

linings. The black-hawk also soars with flat wings, rather than a dihedral. Perched, the black-hawk's tail has a single white band, instead of several thinner bands as in the zone-tailed,

Nesting occurs in tall, streamside trees like cottonwoods. The nest is large, deeply hollowed and made of branches and sticks, and the average number of eggs is two. Little else is known about the zone-tailed hawk's breeding biology, except that it will aggressively defend its nest against intruders.

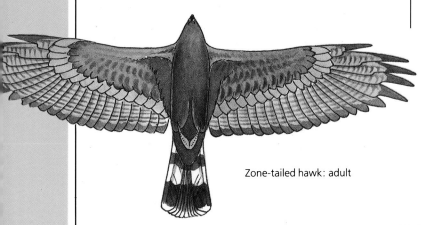

Zone-tailed hawk: adult

IDENTIFICATION

PLUMAGE: Black overall, with white-banded tail and wing feathers, resembles turkey vulture in flight.

DISTRIBUTION: Texas, New Mexico and Arizona.

FOOD: Snakes and lizards, small mammals, frogs.

NEST: Deep cup of sticks, built high in tree along water.

EGGS: 2; whitish, often flecked with brown or lavender.

RED-TAILED HAWK
BUTEO JAMAICENSIS

By far the most abundant and widespread hawk in North America, the red-tailed hawk is absent as a breeding species only from the arctic tundra. Everywhere else, from the arid Southwest to eastern farmland and the conifer forests of Canada, its soaring form and high, descending *ke-e-e-r-r-r* call are common.

The red-tail is a robust, powerful buteo, adapted for taking a wide variety of prey, from mice, birds and reptiles to woodchucks and muskrats. Size differs according to sex and geographic region; a southern male may weigh only two pounds, while a boreal female may tip the scales at nearly twice that. On average, red-tails are roughly two feet long, with a four-foot wingspan.

Red-tails are also the most variably plumaged of North American raptors, with seven different sub-species or color phases (not to mention immature plumages and partial albinism) greatly complicating identification. The "standard" red-tail is the eastern form; adults are brown with light mottling above and white below, with a variable band of dark streaks across the belly and a tail that is brick-red above and pinkish below. Western red-tails have the same basic pattern, but show more rufous on the belly and fine dark barring on the tail – the famous hawk in the Buick automobile ads is a western red-tail. Immatures of both forms look similar to adults, but have brown tails with fine dark bands. Because the reddish tail of the adult is only visible from above, hawk-watchers rely on the belly band (which may not always be present), and dark strips along the leading edge of the wing underside, to make an identification.

Roughly one western red-tail in 10 will be a dark-phase bird, with a solid brown body and a dark chestnut tail; there is also a rufous-phase that is chestnut over much of the body. In the Plains and Southwest there occur three confusing subspecies – the "Krider's," "Fuertes'" and "Harlan's" red-tails, once thought to be separate species. Krider's is the palest of the lot, with an almost white head and whitish

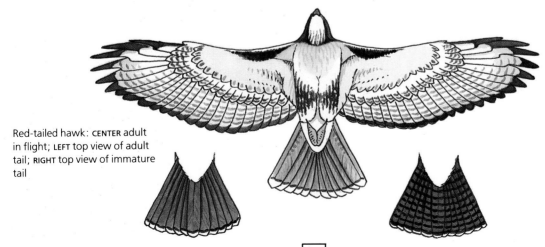

Red-tailed hawk: CENTER adult in flight; LEFT top view of adult tail; RIGHT top view of immature tail

because almost nothing, from rabbits to earthworms, is scorned. For the most part, however, they hunt small to medium-sized mammals like mice, rats, chipmunks, squirrels, rabbits, gophers and ground squirrels, with some birds, snakes and frogs also captured. Individual hawks tend to specialize in certain kinds of prey, depending on what is most abundant in their territory – a red-tail that hunts farmland will have the greatest opportunity to catch mice and rabbits, while one that lives in a wooded area may concentrate on squirrels, woodpeckers, grackles, blue jays and other birds.

Northern red-tails migrate, although by no means do they all do so, and many pairs stay on their territories year-round, perhaps shifting the boundaries a bit to encompass areas that are better hunting through the cold months. They mate, if not for life, then for long periods, and will remember their mate despite a long separation. An albino red-tail in eastern Pennsylvania, which spent five months in a rehabilitation facility recovering from a wing injury, was released in her old territory at the start of the breeding season. She was immediately set upon by her former mate and his new female but within minutes observers noticed that the battle shifted when her mate apparently recognized her. In the end the new female was driven out, and the albino and her old mate settled down to raise another family.

The nest is large and bulky, built high in a tree (or on a cactus or cliff in the West.) The nest may be used year after year, if it is not usurped by a great horned owl, which has the same ecological and habitat requirements as the red-tail. The two or three chicks spend about five weeks in the nest, exercising their wings before finally fledging. A high percentage die in their first year from accidents, starvation and deliberate killing on the part of misguided humans, but the species as a whole seems stable.

tail. Fuertes' looks much like an eastern-red tail, but lacks the belly band and white mottling on the back. Harlan's red-tails are dark, often solid black, with white streaks on the breast and black tails that are mottled or striped with white.

Red-tails can adapt to a wide range of habitats, but are usually found in open country. In the East they are a fixture of rolling farmland, soaring over fields and meadows but nesting in woodlots and forest edges. With the excellent eyesight that is emblematic of hawks, they will kite far above the ground, wings motionless and head down, watching for voles and mice, which they capture after a vertical dive. Other, more wary prey may call for a stealthy approach, and adults in particular will use the terrain to mask a ground-level attack until the last possible second. Red-tailed hawk pairs have even been known to hunt squirrels co-operatively, coming at the animal from opposite sides so it can't use the tree as a shield.

Unlike the highly specialized snail kite, which eats only one thing, the red-tail is a generalist, an opportunist, taking whatever fortune brings its way. A list of red-tailed hawk prey items would be long indeed,

IDENTIFICATION

PLUMAGE: Highly variable. Adult light phase: brown upperparts, white breast with dark belly band, rufous tail. Immature: similar, with brown, dark-banded tail.

DISTRIBUTION: All of North America except arctic.

FOOD: Small mammals, birds, reptiles, amphibians, insects.

NEST: Large, flat and well-made of sticks, high in tree.

EGGS: 2–4; white with often heavy brown spotting.

FERRUGINOUS HAWK
BUTEO REGALIS

The biggest and most powerful of the buteos, the ferruginous hawk of the West is as regal as its Latin name implies. An adult of the normal light-phase is a striking bird – white below, reddish-brown, with rufous thighs that appear as a dark V in flight and a tail of mixed white, gray and russet. There is also a rare dark phase that combines a solid rufous body with white underwing feathers and tail.

Ferruginous (the name means "reddish") hawks are birds of the arid Plains, shortgrass prairies and semi-desert badlands, breeding from Arizona and New Mexico north to Alberta and Saskatchewan; in winter they retreat from the northern half of their range, migrating into California, the border region, Texas and Mexico. They are fairly common, but have declined in recent years, possibly due to illegal shooting.

In many respects, the ferruginous hawk is midway between red-tails and golden eagles in size and behaviour. While only marginally longer than a red-tail, it is substantially heavier, and it hunts with the same rush and vitality that a golden eagle displays. When not on the wing, the ferruginous hawk will often simply sit on the ground, the only buteo to routinely do so.

It is a mammal hunter for the most part, and a pair's territory will usually include one or more large ground squirrel colonies. Unfortunately, ground squirrels are not a constant food source – they hibernate in winter and estivate during the hottest part of summer – so the ferruginous hawk must switch to alternative prey. Jackrabbits and cottontails are often taken, as are prairie dogs, gophers, snakes, sage grouse and prairie chickens. In areas where jackrabbits are

their primary food supply, the number of successful ferruginous hawk nests rises and falls with the predictable population cycle of the hares.

The nest is large and easy to spot, be it in an isolated tree or, just as often, along the edge of a mesa or gully. For some unexplained reason, ferruginous hawks often include chunks of dried horse or cow manure in their nests, presumably a holdover from the days when bison herds roamed these same plains. As with some other Western species, this hawk suffers frequently severe losses of eggs and chicks to the high winds spawned by ferocious thunderstorms.

IDENTIFICATION

PLUMAGE: Rusty upperparts, white underparts, bright rufous thighs. Whitish tail with rusty tip.

DISTRIBUTION: Western Plains.

FOOD: Hares, rabbits, ground squirrels, some birds.

NEST: Very large and messy, of sticks, weeds, often dried dung. In tree or on cliff.

EGGS: 3–5; white background heavily splotched with brown.

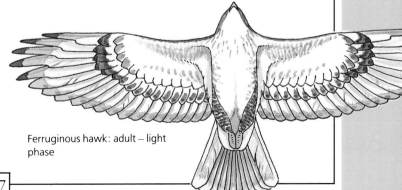

Ferruginous hawk: adult – light phase

ROUGH-LEGGED HAWK
BUTEO LAGOPUS

A common bird of the arctic tundra, the rough-legged hawk would be a cipher to most birders, were it not for the fact that they migrate south in the winter, some wandering as far as Texas and California.

Because they breed in lands far from human habitation, rough-legged hawks are dangerously naive around people, easy to approach and at times almost fearless. In years past a sizable number probably never survived the winter to return to the arctic, but with legal protection and a growing public appreciation for raptors, most are now safe from slaughter.

Rough-leggeds are large buteos, although they are nowhere as powerful as a ferruginous or, for that matter, a red-tail. Their feet, which are feathered to the toes (hence the scientific name, which means "hare-footed hawk") are downright tiny – in keeping with their diet of almost nothing but voles, mice and lemmings. On their southern wintering grounds they stick to open country like the tundra they left behind, hunting from lone trees or on the wing. The rough-legged is one of the only buteos to regularly hover, like a kestrel or an osprey, but the action is far from graceful; the bird looks loose-jointed, as though its flopping wings were about to simply fall off. It will hover for a few moments, either dropping for the attack or sailing off to take up a new position if nothing shows itself.

In flight, a rough-legged hawk has long, rather narrow wings, a broad tail and a strong dihedral that flattens in the primaries. There are two color phases, light and dark, which have long been recognized, but what wasn't widely appreciated until recently is that there are sexual plumage differences as well, making this the only buteo with different male and female plumages. Generally speaking, light phase birds, regardless of age or sex, have dark "elbow" patches on the underside of the wings, a very wide dark belly band and a light tail with a heavy terminal band; adult females are browner, and adult males are mottled with light and dark below. Dark phase birds are solid black, with lighter flight feathers below. Males have white tails with several wide, black bands, while females have only a single black terminal bar.

Because they breed far north of the treeline, rough-legged hawk nests are usually built on cliffs, where they enjoy a degree of safety from ground-dwelling predators like red and arctic foxes. The lemmings and voles on which they depend have dramatic population cycles, which affect breeding success.

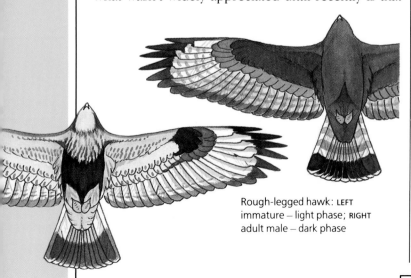

Rough-legged hawk: LEFT immature – light phase; RIGHT adult male – dark phase

IDENTIFICATION

PLUMAGE: Light phase: buffy body with brown head, wide black belly band, dark "wrist" patches and white tail with black terminal band. Dark phase: black body, white tail with multiple dark bands, banded light flight feathers.

DISTRIBUTION: Breeds in arctic; over most of southern Canada and U.S. in winter, except Southwest.

FOOD: Small mammals, a few birds.

NEST: Sticks, weeds, built in tree or on cliff face.

EGGS: 3–8; white often marked with brown

GOLDEN EAGLE
AQUILA CHRYSAETOS

The golden eagle is found over most of the Northern Hemisphere, and wherever it occurs, people have been drawn to it. Its image, cast in metal, led the Roman legions to conquest. Mongol lords used trained eagles to hunt wolves and deer, and Native Americans bestowed its tail feathers on warriors as the ultimate accolade of bravery.

Big, strong and aggressive, the golden eagle is a symbol of wilderness in North America. It is most common in the West, where it inhabits mountains, rimrock and hills, flying out into open country to hunt. Its breeding range extends from the Mexican border and California north to Alaska and east to the Great Plains; a small remnant population still occurs in New England, and an unknown number in eastern Canada.

Golden eagles are large birds, built along the same fluid lines as the bigger buteos, rather than the chunky shape of the bald eagle. The wings are broad and long, stretching roughly 7 feet from tip to tip. The tail is wide and fan-shaped, and the head fairly small and compact. The overall color is a rich brown, tinged with brassy gold on the head and nape. Immature eagles have conspicuous patches of white at the base of the tail and under the wings at the base of the central flight feathers. The patches diminish in size as the bird ages, and by the time the eagle reaches adulthood, the wing patches disappear and the tail is gray, with heavy dark bands.

Unlike the bald eagle, which largely scavenges for food, the golden eagle is a hunter – and a superb one at that. Its most common prey are ground squirrels

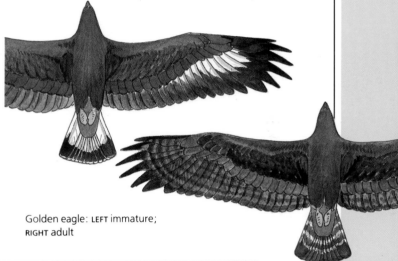

Golden eagle: LEFT immature; RIGHT adult

and jackrabbits, the latter usually caught at the end of a spirited, low-level chase, but a wide variety of small mammals, birds and reptiles are also taken. Neither are golden eagles above eating carrion, especially if natural prey is scarce. This has caused untold deaths among golden eagles, which will feed on poisoned carcasses set out for coyotes. And because eagles will feed on dead sheep, they have gained a reputation for stock-killing. Although a few lambs do die from eagle attacks, the numbers are too small to justify the slaughter that went on in the Southwest, even after golden eagles were granted legal protection in the 1960s. As many as 20,000 were killed in Texas and New Mexico alone between 1940 and 1962, and illegal shootings and poisonings continued long after the law went into effect.

Cliffs are the preferred nest site, with an annual refurbishing of the stick structure adding to a nest's already considerable bulk. Rarely are there more than two or three eggs laid, and because the chicks hatch at different times, the youngest stands a poor chance of surviving the trampling and aggressive behaviour of the oldest chick – the so-called "Cain and Abel syndrome."

The golden eagle is a year-round resident in the West, but in the arctic, and the east, it migrates south for the winter. Along the ridge hawk-watches of the East it is one of the rarest and most treasured migrants; at Pennsylvania's Hawk Mountain Sanctuary (where the presence of eastern golden eagles was first documented in the 1930s,) fall totals rarely exceed 50 or 60 goldens. They are late migrants, not appearing along the ridges until October, and reaching their peak in the bitter winds of November.

IDENTIFICATION

PLUMAGE: Adult: brown overall, with golden neck hackles. Immature: similar, but with white underwing patches and white tail base.

DISTRIBUTION: Western Canada and U.S.; small population in eastern Canada, New England. Rare wintering species in East.

FOOD: Small to medium mammals, birds, reptiles, some carrion.

NEST: Large stick mass on cliff face.

EGGS: 2; one egg usually more heavily marked with brown splotching.

CRESTED CARACARA
POLYBORUS PLANCUS

The caracara is a falcon – but one wouldn't know it from outward appearances. This large, ground-dwelling raptor of the tropics is very much unlike the other sleek members of the falcon family, and its proper relationship to falcons, hawks and eagles has been debated for years. It is now categorized with the falcons based on its notched beak and a number of internal similarities.

A red-tail-sized bird with long wings, neck and very long legs, the caracara is found in the U.S. only in central Florida, Texas and Arizona, then south through Mexico and South America; this is the "eagle" that is revered as Mexico's national bird. A caracara has a large head and heavy bill, a chesty body and a fairly long tail. Adults sport a shaggy black crown, white face (with pink facial skin,) barred chest and black body. In flight, the wings are black, except for white patches on the outermost primaries, and the tail is barred with a heavy terminal band. Immatures are similar but browner. In the air, it is easy to mistake a caracara for a black vulture, although the long tail and big head of the caracara are diagnostic marks.

Caracaras are not active hunters, although they will take birds, rodents, reptiles and amphibians. For the most part they are carrion scavengers, frequently seen along roads picking at highway kills, or harassing vultures into disgorging their meals (hence the colloquial names "king of the vultures" and "king buzzard".) Like the secretary bird of the African plains, the caracara will spring along the ground on its large feet, which lack well-developed talons, running down small animals.

Open country, especially grass- and brushlands and the prairies of Florida, are home to caracaras, but they nest in dense cabbage palmettos or tall pines (cactus in their western range) that provide a good view of the surrounding landscape. The nest is bulky and unlined, holding two or three eggs.

The caracara seems to be declining across its U.S. range, although it remains fairly common in proper habitat in Florida and southern Texas. The Guadalupe caracara, found only on Guadalupe Island off the coast of Baja California, became extinct in 1900, just 25 years after it was discovered. This very dark species (or subspecies) was shot mercilessly by settlers incensed at its attacks on young goats.

IDENTIFICATION

PLUMAGE: Dark body, light head with black crest, banded tail; prominent pink facial skin. White wing patches in flight.

DISTRIBUTION: Central Florida, Texas, extreme southern Arizona.

FOOD: Carrion, small animals.

NEST: Bulky mass of twigs, brush, built in tree or palmetto.

EGGS: 2–3; heavily marked with buff, brown and rust.

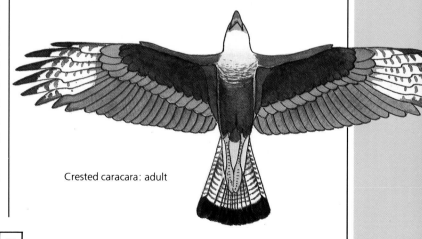

Crested caracara: adult

AMERICAN KESTREL
FALCO SPARVERIUS

Next to the red-tailed hawk, this tiny, colorful falcon has the widest North American breeding range of any of the diurnal raptors. Except for the arctic and a few pockets in southern Florida, Texas and the Pacific Northwest, it is found virtually everywhere.

What is more, this is a bird very much at home with human beings, hunting from telephone wires along country lanes, or snatching grasshoppers scared up by farm machinery. Many nest in the eaves of barns, in abandoned silos and in specially built nesting boxes. Most, however, still prefer an old woodpecker hole or some other natural tree cavity.

Only the size of a mourning dove, the kestrel still retains the aerodynamic shape of the larger falcons. The wings are slim and tapered, the tail long and narrow, the head quite round. Like the northern harrier, the kestrel exhibits profound plumage differences between males and females. Both sexes have a complicated facial pattern of blue-gray, russet and white, with two heavy "moustache" stripes, but where the female is reddish-brown with dark bars on the back, wings and tail, the male has bluish wings and an orange tail with a black terminal band. Further, the female's breast is streaked with rust, while the male's has small black spots.

The kestrel was known for many years as the sparrow hawk, an unfortunate name for several

reasons. It invites confusion with the European sparrowhawk, actually an accipiter very much like the sharp-shinned hawk. Worse, it suggests that the kestrel's main food is birds, which it is not. In summer, this diminutive hawk feeds largely on grasshoppers, crickets, beetles and other large insects, and much of its diet year-round is made up of voles, mice and shrews. It will take a few small birds, as well as snakes,

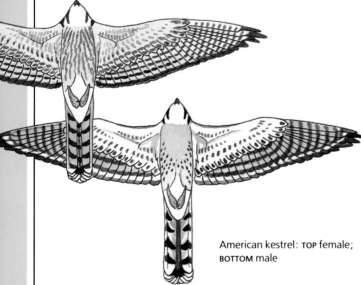

American kestrel: TOP female; BOTTOM male

hovering on rapidly beating wings before dropping to the tall grass for a mouse. In some parts of its range, the East in particular, winter road counts and fall migration tallies indicate that kestrel populations may be dropping for unknown reasons, although it remains the most visible hawk on the continent.

Clutches are large – anywhere from three to seven eggs – indicating that mortality is equally high. Indeed, the average life expectancy is rarely more than 1½ years, and kestrels face a host of dangers. Besides natural predators like raccoons and snakes, which destroy nests, they are hit by cars, shot, die in window collisions, eat poisoned mice and suffer from the effects of pesticides in the food chain.

frogs, lizards and even bats or earthworms. Hunting is done from perches or while hovering, a kestrel speciality.

Although they may be found around spruce bogs in Canada and other forest openings, the kestrel is first and foremost a bird of the open country, particularly farmland. It is one of the birds that benefited greatly from the changes agriculture wrought on the North American continent, and it is undoubtedly more abundant today than it was in presettlement times.

Almost every farm child grew up familiar with its fast, high *klee-klee-klee-klee* call, or the sight of one

IDENTIFICATION

PLUMAGE: Male: blue-gray wings, rusty back and tail, spotted breast. Female: rusty wings, back and tail, barred with black. Both sexes have prominent black facial stripes.

DISTRIBUTION: Virtually all of U.S. and Canada except arctic.

FOOD: Small mammals, insects, some birds, reptiles, amphibians.

NEST: Tree cavity or artifical nest box.

EGGS: 3–5; buffy, with light brown flecking.

MERLIN
FALCO COLUMBARIUS

Merlin: adult

Not much larger than a kestrel, the merlin (formerly known as the pigeon hawk) is a much more aggressive hunter, chasing down songbirds in what can be spectacular aerial contests.

The merlin is primarily a northern breeder, occurring near forest openings across Canada, the northern Rockies, Pacific Northwest and Alaska, in woodlands (and a few towns like Saskatoon) on the Canadian prairies and on the arctic tundra near pockets of trees. The tiaga merlin, which is found in the coniferous forests of the north, is the most widespread form; males are dark blue-gray above and streaked with brown below, while the females are browner overall. Merlins have banded tails, and lack the distinct facial stripes of the kestrel or peregrine falcon. Prairie merlins are lighter in color, and the so-called "black" merlin of the Northwest is very dark, appearing black in all but the best lighting. Immatures are almost identical to females.

A merlin is the falcon equivalent of the sharp-shinned hawk – an agile, bold hunter of small birds. The merlin does not dive from on high, as does the peregrine, but rather relies on surprise, as with accipiters. It will fly low through a forest clearing or along the edge of marsh, rising and falling in a flight pattern similar to a woodpecker's. This may be a form of behavioral minicry, because the merlin's prey might not recognize the approaching bird as a pred-ator until it is too late. When the flock panics and flushes, the merlin lays on the speed, trying to close with and rise above its prey. If it is successful, the merlin drops in a short stoop, ending the chase. Interestingly, merlins have been known to use mankind to their own advantage; in one case, naturalists in Mexico observed six merlins, wintering in the area, pacing a train and catching the birds it flushed.

Although a merlin may take prey as large as a pigeon or a small duck, most of its diet is composed of small- to mid-sized songbirds like sandpipers, warblers, sparrows, blackbirds, jays and woodpeckers. Small mammals, insects (especially dragonflies), reptiles, amphibians and bats are also taken.

Merlins are the most adaptable of North American falcons when it comes to nesting sites. Most pairs use abandoned crow or magpie nests, sometimes adding a further lining of bark and feathers. Others are cavity nesters, choosing appropriately sized woodpecker holes, while still others have nested on cliffs. In tundra areas where trees are scarce, they have even been known to make a shallow scrape in the dirt and lay their eggs directly on the ground.

IDENTIFICATION

PLUMAGE: Male: blue-gray upperparts, heavily streaked buffy breast. Female: similar but browner.

DISTRIBUTION: Breeds in boreal forest across Canada and Alaska, south in prairies to Oregon and Wyoming. Winters in South, Southwest.

FOOD: Primarily songbirds.

NEST: Abandoned hawk nest or tree cavity.

EGGS: 3–5; heavily spotted with brown.

APLOMADO FALCON
FALCO FEMORALIS

This beautifully colored tropical species was once a common breeding bird of the U.S. Southwest, but it has all but vanished from the area, occurring there now only as an accidental visitor.

The aplomado is a medium-sized falcon, roughly midway between a merlin and a peregrine. It is related to the bat falcon of Mexico and Central America, and like that smaller species has a black "waistcoat" that separates the white chest from the rufous thighs and belly. An adult has a dark head and single moustache mark, with a light eyestripe that makes a very good field mark.

As might be expected, the aplomado falcon has been little studied. Biologists were long divided about its primary diet; many early observers in Mexico and Central America considered it sluggish, a lizard and reptile eater, while more recent studies suggest that it is an active bird-hunter – but largely at dawn and dusk, when humans are least likely to notice. Like the merlin it hunts in an accipiter-like fashion, using a low-level approach and cover to surprise its prey at close range. Also like the merlin (and many other hawks) the aplomado falcon has been known to hunt in pairs.

In northern Mexico and the Southwest, old hawk and raven nests are used by breeding aplomado falcons. Three seems to be the normal number of eggs in a clutch.

An officially listed endangered species in the U.S., aplomado falcons are being reintroduced to the wild in Texas, a project begun in 1985. Initial results were not encouraging; of the first four hacked out, two were immediately killed by great horned owls, and the other two so badly harassed by scissor-tailed flycatchers that they had to be recaptured. Between 1985 and 1988, 17 captive-bred falcons were released, however, and plans for a similar project in Arizona, beginning in 1991, raise the hope that this lovely bird will return to its former habitat.

IDENTIFICATION

PLUMAGE: Rusty underparts with black "waistcoat", bold facial pattern, dark underparts.

DISTRIBUTION: Reintroduced to Texas; formerly Arizona.

FOOD: Birds, some small animals.

NEST: Abandoned hawk or crow nest in low tree or shrub.

EGGS: 3; white blotched with chestnut.

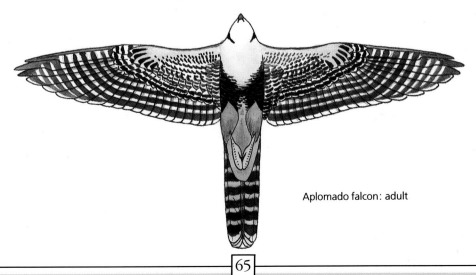

Aplomado falcon: adult

PEREGRINE FALCON
FALCO PEREGRINUS

It is easy to wax poetic about the peregrine falcon – the bird of kings, the fastest creature on earth. The peregrine is all of that, and a good deal more. It is a superb mating of form and function, of beauty and adaptation – and to watch a peregrine in the air is to see magic on the wing.

Unfortunately, finding a peregrine to watch can be difficult. More than any other raptor, the peregrine suffered catastrophic losses after World War II, when chemical pesticides came into wider use. Never common, it all but disappeared from traditional eyries east of the Mississippi, and declined significantly in the West. Even the much larger arctic population has shown signs of pesticide contamination, picked up on their wintering grounds in Central and South America. By 1970, the peregrine was considered extinct as a breeding species in the East, and an endangered species elsewhere.

In response, the Cornell Laboratory of Ornithology's Peregrine Fund started breeding peregrines in captivity, then releasing the chicks to the wild in a modification of an old falconry technique called hacking. Losses of hacked chicks, to accidents, owl predation and starvation, were quite high, but over the years the project's value has been demonstrated. Peregrine falcons again nest in many Northeastern states where they had been absent for more than 30 years, and the population appears to be quickly increasing. Many of the pairs have taken up residence on city skyscrapers or beneath giant bridges, replicating their traditional nesting habitat of cliffs (and with a handy supply of pigeons to eat).

Peregrines are large falcons, bigger than crows. Adults are slate-gray above, with a black head, large

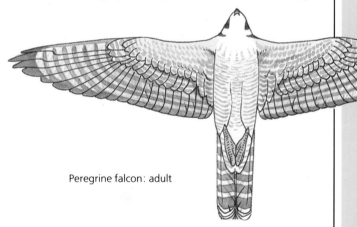

Peregrine falcon: adult

facial "mustache" and barred underparts. Immatures are brown on the back, wings and head, with a brown-streaked breast. Peale's falcon, the peregrine subspecies of the Northwest coast, is very dark, while the tundra birds of the north, most commonly seen in migration along the East coast, are quite a bit lighter.

The peregrine was prized by medieval falconers for its willingness to "wait on," circling high above the falconer and his dogs until prey – usually a grouse, duck or other large bird – is flushed. Then the falcon sideslips into a dive, gaining speed with quick wing-beats, finally drawing its primaries back to form a teardrop shape. The falcon drops like a bolt, hitting speeds of up to 175 mph as it plummets. Special corneal muscles in the eye compensate for the rapidly decreasing distance, allowing the peregrine to keep its prey in sharp focus; special baffles in the nostril permit it to breathe despite the rush of air. Talons extended, the falcon slams into its prey, ripping (or

sometimes almost punching it) as it passes, then flips out of the dive and grabs the falling bird. A peregrine will also simply out-fly its prey in a level, flat-out chase, matching it move for move, cutting the slowest sandpiper or duck from the flock. The spectacle leaves an earthbound human with a slack jaw and weak knees.

IDENTIFICATION

PLUMAGE: Adult: dark gray upperparts, buffy breast with dark barring, banded tail. Heavy "mustache" marks on face. Immature: similar but browner.

DISTRIBUTION: Endangered in East, rare in Western mountains. Widespread in arctic.

FOOD: Small to medium birds.

NEST: None built; scrape on a cliff ledge, under bridge or no skyscraper ledge.

EGGS: Usually 4; heavily blotched and spotted with rusty brown.

PRAIRIE FALCON
FALCO MEXICANUS

In the same arid scrublands of the West where ferruginous and Swainson's hawks live, the prairie falcon haunts the cliffs and rocky hills, hunting for birds and small mammals with almost the same bravado that the peregrine exhibits.

The prairie falcon belongs to the so-called "desert group" of falcons, hot-climate birds that include the lanner falcon of Africa and the saker of the Middle East and Asia. It is nearly as large as the better-known peregrine, with a slimmer body and brown plumage. From below, a flying prairie falcon's best field mark are the very dark patches that stretch from the axillars (or "wingpits") out along the wing linings. From above, the wings appear dark and the tail much lighter, a combination not found in brown, immature peregrines.

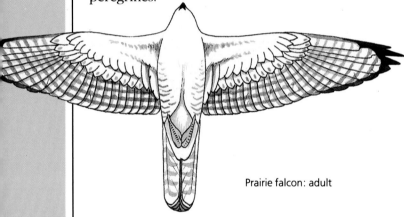

Prairie falcon: adult

During the breeding season, prairie falcons are found from British Columbia east to the Plains, west to the coastal mountains and south to Arizona and New Mexico. They winter over most of the same territory, although some retreat from the extreme northern fringe and others drop down into Texas and Mexico. Within its chosen habitat – dry, open land with buttes, cliffs and badlands – it is a common raptor.

Prairie falcons excel at catching birds in flight, especially larks, doves, sparrows, quail and other ground-dwelling birds that it can startle into suddenly flushing. If rodents are more common, however, the falcon has no hesitation about concentrating its efforts on ground squirrels or prairie dogs. In the Snake River Birds of Prey Area in Idaho, where more than 200 pairs of prairie falcons live along the rugged river canyon, their breeding cycle is timed to coincide with the peak abundance of young ground squirrels.

Prairie falcons are almost strictly cliff nesters, choosing a ledge that offers an overhang for protection from the weather, a flat floor so the eggs won't roll out, a commanding view of the surroundings and a reliable source of food nearby. The female makes a small scrape in the dirt of the ledge floor and lays her four or five eggs with no further preparation.

Although the prairie falcon remains a fairly common species, there are concerns about its future. Many of the areas it inhabits are being opened for mineral production, and the disturbance is bound to have a negative effect on the falcons. In some areas home construction in the foothills where it hunts and breeds has caused local declines, although in other locations, human habitation has had little effect. Fortunately, wildlife agencies now keep a close watch on prairie falcon numbers, and their well-being – and that of wildlife in general – is routinely considered on public lands before habitat disturbance is allowed.

IDENTIFICATION

PLUMAGE: Pale brown above, buffy breast streaked with brown. Long banded tail. Prominent dark wing linings.

DISTRIBUTION: Western prairies and badlands from southern Canada to Mexican border.

FOOD: Birds, small mammals, some reptiles and insects.

NEST: Cliff ledge.

EGGS: 4–5; white, very heavily marked with light brown.

GYRFALCON
FALCO RUSTICOLIS

According to the legendary protocol of ancient falconry, the merlin was flown by ladies, the peregrine by lords – but the gyrfalcon, especially the white gyr, was reserved for a king or emperor.

While in real life that hierarchy may not have been strictly attended to, the gyrfalcon certainly deserves its place at the top. It is the biggest falcon in North America (indeed the world,) a bird of circumpolar distribution and noble bearing. A large female may be two feet long, with wings that stretch across four feet – an imposing predator, especially when matched with typical falcon speed and maneuverability.

The gyrfalcon is a bird of the arctic. In North America it is found from Labrador and the Ungava peninsula of Quebec across the High Arctic islands, the Northwest Territories, the Yukon and Alaska. It inhabits the treeless tundra, nesting on cliffs and eroded river canyons and hunting the flat muskeg for ptarmigan, gulls, shorebirds, waterfowl and the occasional small rodent.

While gyrfalcons come in a range of colors, from pure white to very dark gray, there are too many intergrades for these variations to be considered true "phases." Each color group has its own area of abundance – white gyrs are most common in Greenland and the islands of the Arctic Ocean, the dark birds in the western half of the range, and gray gyrfalcons almost everywhere. Birds of different colors freely interbreed, which further confuses the issue.

With the treeless tundra presenting vistas that go on for miles, the gyrfalcon usually hunts by perching on a high, rocky outcropping and watching for movement below. Far and away the favorite prey is willow ptarmigan, which change from brown to white in winter to mask their presence from the falcon's sharp eyes. If the ruse is unsuccessful, the gyr takes to the air, dropping low to use the terrain to hide its approach. The capture comes after a long chase, rather than a single, overwhelming stoop as with the peregrine.

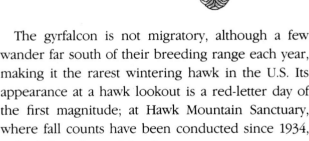

White gyrfalcon

The gyrfalcon is not migratory, although a few wander far south of their breeding range each year, making it the rarest wintering hawk in the U.S. Its appearance at a hawk lookout is a red-letter day of the first magnitude; at Hawk Mountain Sanctuary, where fall counts have been conducted since 1934, only six have been sighted.

IDENTIFICATION

PLUMAGE: Many gradations from almost pure white to solid, sooty gray.

DISTRIBUTION: Arctic tundra near cliffs, river canyons, bluffs.

FOOD: Medium birds, especially ptarmigan, some mammals.

NEST: Old hawk or raven nest, or cliff ledge.

EGGS: Usually 4; whitish, lightly spotted with brown.

COMMON BARN-OWL
TYTO ALBA

If the truth were known, many ghost stories could be laid at the feet of this surpassingly odd bird, which with its silent flight, pale plumage and hellish scream has lifted the hair of lots of night-time travelers, convincing them that they'd experienced a brush with the supernatural.

The most nocturnal of the owls, the barn-owl is placed by biologists in a family all its own – and with good reason. There are many structural differences between barn-owls and other "typical" owls that make up the family Strigidae. The facial disc is heart-shaped rather than round, the central talon of each foot has a peculiar serration along the inner edge, and the legs are very long; at rest, the barn-owl looks to be nothing more than head and legs, with no body in between. For all that it is a lovely bird, with golden plumage shot through with pearly gray above, and ranging from cinnamon to pure white below. The eyes are dark – also unusual for an owl – giving it a soulful gaze.

Barn-owls are cosmopolitan, with 11 species found on every continent except Antarctica. In North America, the common barn-owl (the same species found in Europe) is a southern bird, reaching its farthest limits in Washington state, the central Plains and New York, where severe winters may decimate the population. As the name suggests, barn-owls roost and nest in barns, abandoned buildings, silos, water towers, church steeples – anywhere out of the weather and removed from undue disturbance. They also frequently use hollow trees, but of course such nests are less likely to be found by humans.

Even in the days when hawks and owls in general were considered vermin, barn-owls were highly regarded by farmers, who knew that they killed rats and mice. Biologists later confirmed that belief by studying food pellets coughed up by roosting owls, and discovered that mice – especially meadow voles – may make up 95 percent of this species' diet, although other small mammals and occasionally small birds are also captured. Although the owl may do some hunting around the barn, it relies heavily on grass meadows and uncut hay fields where voles are abundant. It is thought that changing land use practices, especially loss of grasslands and increasing pesticide use, is to blame for the precipitous decline of barn-owls in many areas. Several states, particularly in the Midwest, have listed the barn-owl as threatened or endangered.

Because the barn-owl has a very short life expectancy (less than two years is average,) it has a high reproductive rate to make up the losses. Brood size and frequency is tied to the cyclical vole population, but in a good year a female may lay nearly a dozen eggs in a clutch, and breed virtually year-round. When disturbed, both adults and chicks will spread their wings and swing their lowered heads from side to side – a move called "toe-dusting" – while emitting a hideous, screeching hiss.

IDENTIFICATION

PLUMAGE: Upperparts golden with gray flecks, undersides white or buffy. Heart-shaped facial disc. Brown eyes.

DISTRIBUTION: U.S. except for northern states.

FOOD: Small mammals, occasionally small birds.

NEST: Tree cavities, in barns, silos, abandoned buildings.

EGGS: Up to 12; pure white.

FLAMMULATED OWL
OTUS FLAMMEOLUS

Tiny and rarely seen, the flammulated owl of the West is a ghost of the ponderosa pine forests, tantalizing birders with its faint hoot, but only infrequently seen.

For years, bird-watchers and experts alike considered the flammulated owl a rare bird, but more recent studies show it to be one of the most common raptors within its habitat – just one that is very good at avoiding human eyes. A member of the screech-owl complex of species, the flammulated is a Lilliputian hunter, scarcely six inches long, with doll-sized talons and dark eyes. Like the other screech-owls it has small ear tufts and mottled plumage that provide excellent camouflage against the peeling bark of a pine tree. There are two color phases, gray and red, the latter with a bright rusty facial disc and a row of reddish spots along the scapulars, or back feathers; this explains the name flammulated, which means "flame-bearer."

It is unusual to find a flammulated owl outside the ponderosa pine forests of the western mountains, from the Southwest up through Idaho, Washington and extreme southern British Columbia. A highly migratory species, the owl arrives from its Mexican and Central American wintering grounds in May and sets up a territory that includes one or more woodpecker holes.

"Territory" may be too precise a word, since flammulated owls sometimes nest in loose colonies, and in good habitat may be found at a rate of five or six pairs per square mile. The three or four eggs are incubated for about 3½ weeks, and the chicks, once hatched, are fed on insects, especially moths and caterpillars, but also beetles, crickets and even scorpions.

Although it is apparently more common than once thought, the flammulated owl's future is cloudy. Ponderosa pine is a vulnerable lumber species, and is heavily logged in many parts of the West. Because it breeds almost completely in ponderosa stands, the welfare of the flammulated owl will hinge on wise management of the forests.

IDENTIFICATION

PLUMAGE: Mottled browns, russets, grays, with reddish scapular feathers on back. Some birds grayer. Small ear tufts, brown eyes.

DISRIBUTION: Ponderosa pine forests from Rockies west.

FOOD: Insects.

NEST: Old woodpecker holes.

EGGS: 2–4; white.

EASTERN SCREECH-OWL
OTUS ASIO

Deep forests, farm woodlots, city parks and suburban backyard – anywhere there are large trees for nesting, the eastern screech-owl can call home. It is probably the most common owl within its range, which extends from the Plains and Texas to the Atlantic coast and southern Canada.

About as large as a man's fist, the screech-owl is a small lookalike for the much bigger great horned owl, and is often mistaken for a baby of that species. But a full-grown screech barely exceeds 8 inches, from its small "ear" tufts to its short tail. The face is round, with a dark line surrounding the facial disc, and a mottled pattern of light and dark on the breast. The color is highly variable. There are two or three phases (depending on who is counting) – a red phase, actually brick-orange; a gray phase; and a brown phase that some authorities simply lump with the gray.

The color phases are not tied to age or sex, but there does seem to be a correlation to climate and, possibly, habitat. Gray phase birds tend to be more common in the northern portion of the screech-owl's range, and experiments indicate that they are more tolerant of cold temperatures than the red-phase birds to the south, which need more food in winter. Field studies in Ohio, where both morphs occur, showed that red-phase owls decreased significantly after severe winters, while gray-phase birds fared better. Why this should be is still unanswered, however.

Eastern screech-owls are difficult to see during the day, but their distinctive "whinny" call, a quavering, descending whistle, is a sure tip-off to their presence.

Courtship begins in late winter and very early in spring, and nesting, which takes place in a hollow tree or large birdbox, is accomplished by the time most migratory birds are just arriving for the spring. Family size varies from two or eight, depending on the age of the adults and the abundance of food. Screech owls are analogous to kestrels, in that they hunt for large insects like moths, grasshoppers and katydids, mice, frogs, snakes, salamanders and other small animals.

For their small size, screech-owls can be fearsome defenders of their nests. This attribute is all well and good if the intruder is a raccoon bent on egg-stealing, but what often happens is that the owls nest near a busy sidewalk or jogging path, then terrorize passersby. Unlike some birds that merely dive without striking, screech-owls will not hesitate to rake a person's head with those needle-sharp talons. Because they are legally protected, the best recourse is to choose a new route for a few weeks, or carry an umbrella.

IDENTIFICATION

PLUMAGE: Two phases, red and gray. Cryptic streaks and blotches on breast. Small ear tufts.

DISTRIBUTION: Plains east to Atlantic, southern Canada to Texas.

FOOD: Small mammals, insects, some birds, reptiles, amphibians.

NEST: Tree cavity or artificial nest box.

EGGS: 4–6; white.

WESTERN SCREECH-OWL and WHISKERED SCREECH-OWL
ASIO KENNECOTI AND ASIO TRICHOPSIS

Superficially, all three species of screech-owls – the eastern, western and whiskered – look alike. All have short ear tufts, cryptically colored plumage and yellow eyes; in fact, the eastern and western cannot safely be separated by appearance. But all three have markedly different calls, and because they do not interbreed with each other, they have been accorded status as distinct species.

The western screech-owl was lumped with the eastern as one species until a few years ago, when it was "split," in the parlance of birders. It occupies much the same sort of habitat as its eastern cousin, especially oak woodlands, orchards and deciduous groves. There is less variation in color, with most birds being gray, except for the Northwest coast, where brown is the most prevalent hue.

The western screech-owl's call is very different from the eastern's whinny. There are two common calls, a series of accelerating notes on the same pitch, and a short, then long, trill. In most respects the breeding biology is the same as the eastern screech-owl.

The whiskered screech-owl is marginally smaller than the western, with abundant bristles around the mouth – the "whiskers" of its name. Unlike the widespread western screech-owl, the whiskered is restricted in the U.S. to southeastern Arizona and southwest New Mexico, in mountain oak forests up to about 4,000 feet in elevation. A cavity nester, the whiskered screech-owl has been little studied, although it seems likely that its life history is similar to its more common counterparts. As with the western, its call is the best identifying clue, a long string of short hoots or a "Morse Code" series of irregularly spaced notes.

IDENTIFICATION

PLUMAGE: Almost identical to gray-phase eastern screech-owl, but with different call.

DISTRIBUTION: West from Plains to Pacific, Pacific Northwest south to Mexican border.

FOOD: Small mammals, insects, reptiles, amphibians, small birds.

NEST: Tree or cactus cavity.

EGGS: 2–5; white.

IDENTIFICATION

PLUMAGE: Almost identical to western screech-owl, but with abundant mouth bristles, greenish bill base. Call best distinguishing mark.

DISTRIBUTION: Southeastern Arizona.

FOOD: Insects.

NEST: Tree cavity.

EGGS: 3–4; white.

GREAT HORNED OWL
BUBO VIRGINIANUS

If there were a prize for most successful predator, the great horned owl would likely win hands-down. Not only is it found in virtually every corner of North America, it is equally at home in the rain forests of Central America and the frigid climate of Tierra del Fuego at the southernmost tip of South America, and everywhere in between. It nests in desert cactus, hunts snowshoe hares in the Canadian woods and patrols city dumps for rats – truly an owl for all seasons.

This adaptive wonder is the familiar hoot owl of childhood, whose round face and upright ear tufts appears on Halloween decorations and in horror movies. The real thing is harder to find, even though it is common over all of its range. About two feet long, with a wingspan of up to five feet, it is exceeded in size only by the snowy owl and the great gray owl – and the great gray is mostly feathers. A four-pound female great horned owl is immensely powerful, able to handle even fairly large mammals like opossums and young raccoons. The plumage is an intricate mix of browns, white and black, mottled on the back and barred on the breast, which helps the owl to blend perfectly with its surroundings.

Like the red-tailed hawk (which has many of the same habitat requirements,) the great horned owl is a generalist. Its prey may include virtually any creature small enough to be caught and killed, and local abundance plays more of a role in determining an individual owl's diet than any other factor. If meadow voles and house mice are the easiest to catch, then the great horned will focus on them. Along rivers, they may take mostly muskrats, snakes, frogs and fish; a forest-dwelling owl will be forced by circumstance to concentrate on flying squirrels, rabbits and songbirds.

Great horned owls are usually the first species of bird to begin breeding each year. In the latitude of Pennsylvania, pairs will be calling to each other in courtship by early January, and will have picked out an old crow, hawk or squirrel nest a few weeks later. The eggs – usually two or three – are laid by mid-February, and hatch a month or so later. The chicks are kept warm and dry by the solicitous female, who broods constantly for the first few weeks as the much smaller male works overtime to bring in food. By April the young will be fairly large, still flightless and downy but beginning to explore their surroundings. At this stage, many clamber out onto nearby branches, or jump to the ground. So protective are the parents that even the wanderers usually survive.

The early breeding season is essential so that the chicks have the entire summer – when young, dumb prey animals are abundant – to learn how to hunt. The family will stay together through the fall and early winter, only separating when another breeding season rolls around.

The clear, deep call of the great horned owl is one of the best-known sounds of the night woods – a series of six or seven low hoots, somewhat higher pitched in the female than in the male. A pair will call antiphonally for hours, especially while courting.

IDENTIFICATION

PLUMAGE: Upperparts richly mottled in brown, white, buff and black, undersides buffy with horizontal barring. Reddish facial disc, large ear tufts.

DISTRIBUTION: All of North America except treeless tundra.

FOOD: Wide variety of mammals, birds, reptiles, amphibians, insects, fish.

NEST: Abandoned nest of hawk or other bird, sometimes in hollow of broken tree branch, cave or cliff ledge.

EGGS: Usually 2; white.

SNOWY OWL
NYCTEA SCANDIACA

An airport would seem to be an unlikely place to look for rare owls, but each winter, snowy owls that wander south from the arctic end up at airports in Northeastern cities like Boston and Toronto, sometimes by the dozen. The flat, grassy taxiways apparently remind the owls of the tundra – and although there are no jumbo jets on the muskeg, they seem undisturbed by the constant roar of turbines.

Most of the time, the snowy owl lives far beyond mankind's pale, with caribou, muskoxen and polar bears for neighbours. They breed on the rolling coastal plain of the Arctic Ocean, where constant sunlight in summer alternates with 24-hour darkness in winter. It is a brutal environment in which to live, but the owl has adapted to it well. It is large – up to four pounds – because a large body retains heat better than a smaller body. It is completely encased in thick feathers, right down to the toes and the pads of the feet. Winter's cold holds no terrors for the snowy owl.

Starvation does, however. Its prey, lemmings and arctic hares, are subject to the population cycles so common among northern herbivores. When the low point is reached and there is little food to go around, the older, more entrenched birds hold the best territories, and the younger owls will be forced to wander south. They may wind up as far down-range as Alabama or even Bermuda, but most go no further than the upper Midwest, New England or southern Canada. They pass the winter on open grassland, farm country or along the coast, areas similar to the open tundra they left behind. They can be absolutely fearless around humans, perching nonchalantly on barn roofs or television antennas, and even the threat of prosecution does not deter some who still can't resist taking a potshot at such a big bird. At one time, it was thought that virtually none of the wintering snowies survived man's unkind attentions. Fortunately, that is changing, and a snowy owl today is more likely to attract hordes of excited birders than a .22 slug.

A snowy owl is so universally recognized that it seems redundant to describe it. Adult males are the whitest, with females showing a fair bit of barring and immatures the most heavily marked of all. The nest is a depression on a raised hummock, above the soggy tundra, with little or no lining. The lemming population directly determines the number of eggs; if food is scarce the owls might not come into breeding condition at all, but during a lemming peak as many as 13 eggs have been recorded in a single nest – clearly a case of making the best of a good situation.

IDENTIFICATION

PLUMAGE: White with varying amounts of black barring; males whitest, juveniles most heavily marked.

DISTRIBUTION: Arctic coastal plain, treeless tundra.

FOOD: Small mammals, hares, birds.

NEST: Depression in low hummock, sometimes lined with feathers.

EGGS: 1—13, depending on food supply; white.

NORTHERN HAWK-OWL
SURNIA ULULA

If the harrier is a hawk that thinks it is an owl, then this north-woods species is an owl that thinks it's a hawk. The hawk-owl has no qualms about hunting in daylight, perched at the top of a tall spruce, long tail wagging, watching for a mouse. When it spots its prey it does not swoop down with the fluttery flight typical of owls, but attacks with a fast, flapping glide more like an accipiter's. It will hover like a kestrel, and obviously relies more on sight than hearing to find its prey. It is, all in all, a very unusual owl.

It is also one that few birders get the chance to see, for it lives in the forests of Canada and Alaska, where open bogs and old fire burns mix with dense stands of spruce and fir. Even there it is not common, although it is conspicuous because of its diurnal habits and tendency to perch in the open.

The hawk is about 16 inches long (a bit shorter for males). Its tapering tail is the most reliable field mark, along with the barred breast and very dark border around the facial discs. The eyes and beak are yellow. Most of the year it is silent, except for a trill on the breeding grounds and an angry *keek-keek-keek-keek* that is similar to the alarm call of . . . a hawk.

Mice and lemmings make up the bulk of the hawk-owl's diet in summer, along with the young of snow-shoe hares, chipmunks and other mammals. In winter, when the rodents burrow safely beneath the snow, it switches over to birds, and despite its only medium size will tackle ptarmigan, grouse and other hefty forest birds, in addition to smaller songbirds.

Like most of the northern owls, the hawk-owl is beguilingly tame; it is not unusual to be able to walk up underneath one, drawing only a half-curious glance from the unconcerned bird. Unlike the snowy owl, hawk-owls rarely wander south of their breeding range, and when one does show up in New England or the Great Lakes region, serious birders from around the country drop what they're doing to see the rarity.

IDENTIFICATION

PLUMAGE: Horizontal barring on undersides, dark upperparts spotted with white, very long, barred tail, square head and black facial disc borders. No ear tufts.

DISTRIBUTION: Boreal forests across Canada, Alaska.

FOOD: Small mammals in summer, more birds in winter.

NEST: Tree cavities or abandoned hawk or crow nests.

EGGS: 4–7; white.

NORTHERN PYGMY-OWL
GLAUCIDIUM GNOMA

Even for an aggressive predator like the northern pygmy-owl, the woods hold dangers. Only 7 inches long, this western owl is at risk even from other owls, like the great horned, which would not hesitate to make a meal of it.

So to fool potential predators, the pygmy-owl has eyes in the back of its head – literally. On the nape of the neck, the owl has two black spots, rimmed with white, that may serve to unnerve attackers. This is a common ruse among moths, butterflies and fish, and it apparently works well for the pygmy-owl as well.

Hardly bigger than a sparrow, the pygmy-owl nevertheless tackles songbirds its own size and even larger, although much of its diet is mammalian, primarily mice. In summer large beetles and grasshoppers are also eagerly hunted.

Often described as diurnal, the pygmy-owl is more properly a crepuscular hunter, most active in the twilight of dawn and dusk. It lacks an important adaptation for night-time hunting that most other owls possess – soft wing feathers to muffle the sound of flight – because it relies on speed and agility to catch its prey, instead of surprise.

The northern pygmy-owl is fairly common in deciduous and mixed forests in the mountains and hills from New Mexico, Arizona and California, north from the eastern slopes of the Rockies to British Columbia and west to the Pacifiç, usually between 5,000 and 10,000 feet of elevation. The basic plumage is rusty brown above with light spots, and a heavily streaked breast; the tail is long and banded. Some individuals are grayer, although the differences may be too slight to justify calling it a color phase. The call is a series of whistled hoots.

The pygmy-owl is a cavity-nester, usually taking over an old woodpecker hole 15 or 20 feet up the tree. As the female incubates her clutch, and later as the three or four chicks grow, the male has responsibility for supplying the food. If he gets a lucky streak, or if he makes a kill that is larger than the family can eat at once, the leftovers may be cached for later eating.

IDENTIFICATION

PLUMAGE: Reddish or gray phases; both have long, light-barred tails, tuftless heads, streaked breasts and black "eye spots" on nape of neck.

DISTRIBUTION: Mountain forests from Rockies west.

FOOD: Small mammals, insects, small birds.

NEST: Woodpecker hole within 20 feet of ground.

EGGS: 3–4; white.

FERRUGINOUS PYGMY-OWL
GLAUCIDIUM BRASILIANUM

Probably the rarest of North America's owls, the ferruginous pygmy-owl is found in small numbers in only a few locations in Arizona and south Texas.

It was not always so rare. In the 1800s it was fairly common over a much larger portion of southern Arizona, and was numerous along the Rio Grande in Texas. But this subtropical raptor needs riparian forests of mesquite, cottonwood and catclaw acacia, which have been largely cleared for agriculture and water management. Most researchers believe the handful of ferruginous pygmy-owls still living north of the Mexican border are doing so in substandard habitat, and are in danger from further brush-clearing operations. Even its status in the core of its range, Mexico, is uncertain.

The ferruginous pygmy-owl looks very much like its more widespread relative the northern pygmy-owl. Both have round, tuftless heads, yellow eyes, black "eye" spots on the back of the neck, and long tails. But while the northern's tail is banded with brown and white, the ferruginous' is brown and black. The call is the most diagnostic feature, a series of *puk-puk* notes, unlike the northern's low hoots.

Insects, scorpions, mice and small birds form this owl's diet. Its nesting behavior is similar to the northern pygmy-owl's, with a woodpecker hole in a tree or large cactus being used, often in successive years.

It is hard to say what the future holds for the ferruginous pygmy-owl, but its survival in the U.S. obviously hinges on human concern. Wildlife managers are trying to protect and expand the fragments of habitat that still remain, to give the surviving few owls a chance. Its fate is a lesson in basic conservation, for no animal can survive without the proper habitat.

IDENTIFICATION

PLUMAGE: Similar to northern pygmy-owl but redder, with dark-banded tail.

DISTRIBUTION: Extreme southern Texas and Arizona.

FOOD: Insects, scorpions, small mammals and birds.

NEST: Tree or cactus cavity.

EGGS: 3–1; white.

ELF OWL
MICRATHENE WHITNEYI

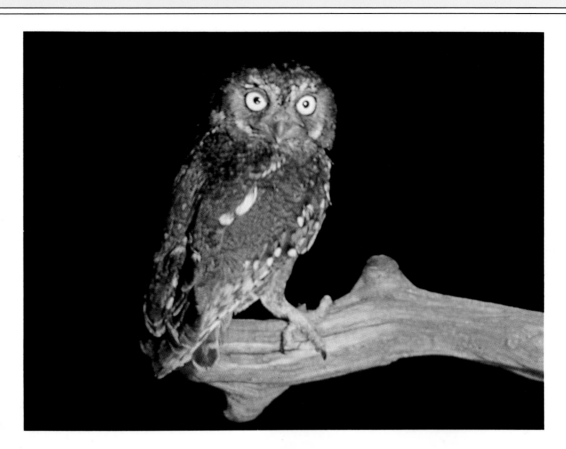

At 1¼ ounces, the elf owl is outweighed by most of the songbirds with which it shares the desert. It is the smallest owl in the world, less than 6 inches long – as small as the moths on which it feeds.

A migratory species that winters in central Mexico and Texas (where it is now rare); it has declined drastically in the California desert, where a reintroduction project is underway. In Arizona, however, it remains abundant, and its shockingly loud *yip* is a common sound as dusk comes to the desert.

The elf owl is easily separated from both pygmy-owls by its very short tail. The head is round and lacks ear tufts, the large eyes are yellow and the body a mottling of buff and gray.

Although the elf owl is found in riparian thickets and oak-pine forests up to 7,000 feet, it is most closely associated with the desert "forests" of saguaro cactus. Here, gila woodpeckers and flickers excavate cavities in the cacti, providing second-hand housing for the owls. The males, which return from Mexico first in the spring, set up territories that include several such holes, then call from the entrances to lure prospective mates. Once a hole is selected there is no further modification; the female simply lays her 2–4 eggs on the floor of the cavity. Even before the eggs hatch, and continuing until the young are nearly fledged, the female will roost in the hole, often watching the desert from its opening. In fact, one of the best ways of spotting an elf owl is by carefully scrutinizing every hole in a saguaro for a small, round face.

In keeping with its size, the elf owl is an insect hunter, taking a wide array of invertebrates, especially large moths, beetles and crickets. It is known for catching dangerous scorpions, which it disarms with a nimble bite to the tail stinger before it eats them.

IDENTIFICATION

PLUMAGE: Sparrow-sized; tuftless head, buffy under-parts, short tail.

DISTRIBUTION: Deserts, canyons and foothills of Arizona, southwest New Mexico and Texas.

FOOD: Insects and arthropods.

NEST: Woodpecker hole in cactus or tree.

EGGS: 2–3; white.

BURROWING OWL
ATHENE CUNICULARIA

On the Plains and through the Southwest, the summer can be a season of vicious, grinding heat for anything unlucky enough to be caught in the sun. Many animals find relief by escaping underground – and that's exactly the tactic used by the burrowing owl, one of the more unusual raptors in North America.

About 9 or 10 inches long, burrowing owls spend most of their time on or near the ground, explaining their longer-than-normal legs. They lack ear tufts on their very rounded heads, have rust-barred underparts and brown backs and wings; juveniles fresh out of the nest have buffy underparts and a broad, dark bib.

Although chiefly nocturnal, burrowing owls are frequently active in the daytime, and their habit of living in vacant lots, golf courses and near airports brings them in regular contact with people. They are particularly fond of prairie dog colonies, an association that stretches far back in time. Prairie dogs – actually rodents – dig extensive networks of tunnels that, in presettlement times, covered hundreds of square miles. The tunnels, in turn, provided homes and food for many other animals, including prairie rattlesnakes, black-footed ferrets and burrowing owls. An old myth holds that the prairie dogs, rattlesnakes and owls live in perfect harmony, but the truth is much less charming; the snakes and the owls will gladly kill young prairie dogs – and that is all the ferrets eat.

Burrowing owls are found from Texas to California, north through western Washington, the northern Plains and southern fringe of the Canadian prairies. There is also a separate, nonmigratory population in southern Florida that is in a disturbing decline.

Burrowing owls have the largest normal broods of any North American owl, often 8 or 9 chicks, sometimes up to a dozen. Insects and rodents make up the bulk of the bird's diet.

IDENTIFICATION

PLUMAGE: Long legs, short tail, tuftless head. Chestnut barring on undersides, back heavily spotted. Juvenile has unmarked, buffy breast.

DISTRIBUTION: Open country from Canadian Plains to California, Texas. Small population in southern Florida.

FOOD: Insects and arthropods, small mammals, lizards, birds.

NEST: Abandoned burrow of prairie dog, badger, gopher, tortoise, other digger. May be enlarged or dug entirely by owl.

EGGS: 6–8, often more; white.

SPOTTED OWL
STRIX OCCIDENTALIS

With its gentle brown eyes and soft plumage, the spotted owl hardly looks like a candidate for controversy. But this beautiful bird of the western mountains has generated a storm of protest, setting environmentalists against loggers in the battle for its forest home.

Spotted owls are found only in old-growth forests, stands of ancient trees, some of which are more than 500 years old. Such trees are prized by timbering interests, and the remaining old-growth stands are disappearing rapidly – and with them, the owl. In the Pacific Northwest, the spotted owl has landed at the center of the battle for these magnificent woodlands. Bowing to industry pressures, the government refused to list the spotted owl as threatened under the Endangered Species Act, despite clear evidence that the owl is in trouble; to do so would mean severe curtailment of timber sales on public land, which includes most of the remaining old-growth. Only after environmental groups took court action did the U.S. Fish and Wildlife Service reverse itself in 1989 and decide to list the owl.

The spotted owl is rather large, very similar to the more widespread barred owl except for spots, rather than vertical barring, on the belly. In addition the Pacific Northwest, it is found in disjunct distribution through the Sierras, southern Rockies and South-

western mountains. Because of logging, its habitat is increasingly fragmented, isolating small populations that may lack the genetic viability for survival.

Small mammals make up most of its diet, especially flying squirrels, mice, wood rats and the red tree vole, which spends its entire life far above the ground in the lichen-covered branches of the great trees. The spotted owl nests in tree cavities and old raptor nests, usually raising just two chicks a season.

IDENTIFICATION

PLUMAGE: Brown above, heavily spotted with white, undersides barred and spotted with brown. No ear tufts, brown eyes.

DISTRIBUTION: Old-growth forests on Pacific coast, Sierras and Southwestern mountains.

FOOD: Flying squirrels, tree voles, other small mammals.

NEST: Tree cavities, abandoned hawk nests, cliff ledges.

EGGS: 2–3; white.

GREAT GRAY OWL
STRIX NEBULOSA

Huge in appearance, the great gray owl is actually a lightweight compared to the great horned and snowy owls – but it is impressive nonetheless, nearly 30 inches long, with a five-foot wingspan.

The great gray is a confirmed northerner, found in the deep conifer forests from central Alaska to Ontario, and in small numbers down through the northern Rockies, Cascades and Sierras at high elevations. Even where it occurs it is a hard bird to see – fading, wraithlike, into the forest.

Tastes vary, but the great gray owl may well be the most attractive of North America's night hunters. Gray, black, white and brown blend with watercolor softness on its plumage, forming streaks, swirls and bars that break up its outline against the backdrop of trees. The face is enormous, with concentric dark rings on the facial discs framing two bright yellow eyes that seem dwarfed in comparison. Two thin white strips at the chin look like a high Victorian collar. The tail is quite long, but the overall impression is that the owl is mostly head.

For its size, the great gray is not a strong hunter, and restricts itself mostly to rodents and squirrels, although it will capture snowshoe hares and rabbits. It often hunts at dawn and dusk, and when there are chicks to feed the adults may forage off and on throughout the day. Old hawk, crow and raven nests

are taken over and deepened to accommodate the owl's two or three eggs, although the rotted top of a broken tree trunk may also be used.

Great gray owls do not migrate, but a few wander south each year, and major irruptions occur on a 10- to 15-year schedule. Those that winter near towns may be so harassed by birders that they are unable to hunt – although the visiting humans sometimes bring a bribe. Wildlife photographers frequently release mice and voles near the owls, hoping for action shots. The owls are so completely fearless of humans, however, that it is not uncommon for the bird to try to take the rodent from a person's hand as soon as it sees food.

IDENTIFICATION

PLUMAGE: Cryptic blend of grays, browns and white. Large, round head, no ear tufts, concentric rings on facial discs, long tail.

DISTRIBUTION: Boreal forests from Alaska to Ontario, south in northern Rockies, Cascades, Sierras.

FOOD: Small mammals.

NETS: Abandoned hawk nest or snapped off tree trunk.

EGGS: 3–5; white.

BARRED OWL
STRIX VARIA

One of the weirdest night sounds to be heard is the nocturnal chorus of a barred owl pair, hooting, moaning and yodeling – it even raises the hair on the neck of a birder who *knows* it's just an owl. No wonder one of this species' old names was the crazy owl.

Common over the East, southern Canada and the northern Rockies, the barred owl is an inhabitant of deep, moist forests – the same habitat where red-shouldered hawks are found. In fact, the owls and the hawks eat much the same prey (small mammals, reptiles, amphibians, crayfish and some birds,) and barred owls will forsake tree cavities to lay their eggs in old red-shouldered nests.

Barred owls are somewhat smaller than great horned owls, about 20 inches from head to the tip of the rather long tail. The head is very round, with faint circles radiating out from the large, brown eyes. The throat and chest are barred horizontally, while the belly has vertical striping; the back is a camouflaging mix of brown, gray and white.

Because they are highly vocal, it is easy to determine if barred owls are in the neighbourhood. Their standard hoot is loud and ringing, usually set down as *Who-cooks-for-you, who-cooks-for-you-a-a-a-allll*, falling off sharply at the end, but the barred owl has a whole repertoire of yelps, barks, caws and screams. They will readily answer a tape recording or even a good vocal imitation, but avoid doing so during the breeding season, when the adults would be distracted from feeding and guarding their young. Imitating a small owl, like a screech-owl or saw-whet, may also pull in a barred owl, for they are not above eating their smaller relatives.

Nesting usually takes place near a swamp, stream or river. As mentioned, a tree cavity is the preferred site, and two or three chicks is the average clutch size.

IDENTIFICATION

PLUMAGE: Brown with heavy white spotting above; white breast with vertical streaking and horizontal barring on chest. No ear tufts, brown eyes.

DISTRIBUTION: Eastern forests and swamps from Gulf Coast to southern Canada, west through Canada to British Columbia, Oregon, Washington.

FOOD: Small mammals, reptiles, amphibians, crayfish, some birds.

NEST: Tree cavity or abandoned hawk or crow nest, especially red-shouldered hawk nest.

EGGS: 2–3; white

LONG-EARED OWL
ASIO OTUS

Take a great horned owl and stretch it like taffy, and you'll have a close approximation of the long-eared owl, a slim "eared" species found over most of the continent.

Despite its wide distribution (absent only from the Deep South and Arctic,) the long-eared owl is one of the most retiring of birds, making it very difficult to locate. It is strongly nocturnal, and spends its days quietly roosting in heavy cover, where its cryptic plumage of buff and brown help it to vanish from sight. Often the only clue to its presence are disgorged food pellets and white droppings on the ground. Look for these signs in thick stands of conifers, where long-eared owls roost in winter, or mixed forests where they breed. Once pellets are found, scrutinize the trees nearby for the owl, which will be perched close to the trunk. When an intruder is around, the owl stretches to its full height, erects its long ear tufts and closes its eyes, all adding to the camouflage – and the difficulty for a birder.

Meadow voles, deer mice, short-tailed shrews, young rats and other small mammals make up the majority of its diet, with a few songbirds plucked from their roosts, frogs, snakes, and insects rounding it out. Pellets composed of nothing but deer hair suggest they may occasionally feed on road-kills, although such behavior does not seem to be common.

Long-eared owls nest in the abandoned nests of hawks, crows and other large birds, as well as the leafy nests of gray squirrels. The adults mount a spirited defense of the nest if a predator comes too close, dive-bombing it, screaming at it and trying to lure it away with a convincing broken-wing act.

In some parts of its range, the long-eared owl appears to be less common than once thought, at least as a breeding species. The Pennsylvania Breeding Bird Atlas, which censused nesting species in every corner of the state, found far fewer long-eared owl nests than had been expected. The species seems to be more common – or at least easier to locate – in the West.

IDENTIFICATION

PLUMAGE: Mix of brown, buff, black similar to great horned owl but smaller, slimmer body, with longer ear tufts.

DISTRIBUTION: Breeds across mid-section of U.S. and southern Canada, retreating south in winter. Uncommon in East.

FOOD: Small mammals, birds.

NEST: Abandoned crow, hawk, squirrel nest.

EGGS: 4–5; white.

SHORT-EARED OWL
ASIO FLAMMEUS

Owls as a group are woodland birds, but the short-eared owl has abandoned the forests for the grasslands and tundra, where it hunts for mice beneath the wide open sky.

Because it lives where trees are scarce, the short-eared is an active hunter, eschewing the quiet wait on a perch that most owls practice. It is up and around before dusk, and hunts past sunrise, so it is often seen flying low over fields and marshes. Its flight is buoyant and mothlike, with fluttering wingbeats interspersed with long glides. In the air, the owl's buffy color and dark "wrist" patches on the undersides of the wings, as well as its round, neckless head, distinguish it from the northern harriers that hunt the same terrain.

The short-eared owl is about 15 inches long, streaked with brown and ocher to blend with dead grass. The ear tufts are very small, invisible at a range of more than a few feet, giving the owl a smooth head that may cause it to be confused with the much whiter barn owl.

Short-eared owls are found in every state and province, but their distribution is spotty and local. They are most common in the West, Midwest and Canada, and much less so in the East. Northern birds migrate south for the winter, when their range drops through the Southwest, Gulf states and South. Watch for them on freshwater and coastal marshes, fallow fields and around large airports. In winter they are gregarious, and if rodents are especially common it is not unusual to find flocks of 20 or more in a small area, roosting companionably on haystacks or muskrat lodges.

The nest is a crude, grass-lined scrape in thick vegetation, sometimes as part of a small colony but most often alone. Like the harrier, its nesting success and clutch size are tied with the rise and fall of vole populations.

IDENTIFICATION

PLUMAGE: Buffy overall, with vertical breast streaking, mottled back.

DISTRIBUTION: Breeds near grasslands or marshes from arctic south to New Jersey, Midwest, Colorado, winters south to Florida and Mexican border. Spotty distribution in East.

FOOD: Small mammals, some birds, insects.

NEST: Depression on ground among heavy grass and weeds.

EGGS: 5–7; white.

BOREAL OWL
AEGOLIUS FUNEREUS

Sharing the woods with the great gray and hawk-owl, the boreal owl is another tame northern species, found in Alaska, Canada and in alpine forests in the Rockies.

The boreal is a small owl, about 9 or 10 inches long, with a large head. The facial discs are surrounded with a heavy black line, there is white spotting on the

back, and the breast is streaked with brown. It is similar to the smaller, more southerly saw-whet owl, but has a yellow (rather than black) bill and a head that is more square than round.

The boreal owl's preferred habitat is dense forests of spruce, fir and birch, where it hunts around bogs and other openings. Daytime roosts are usually deep in a tangle of branches, or even inside a building. They are said to have sheltered in old igloos in the Far North, but since the building of ice houses is a skill rarely practiced in this day of prefab shelters, it seems likely few boreal owls have the chance anymore. Mice and other rodents comprise most of its food, with songbirds in the winter and, in summer, some insects.

The boreal owl is dependent on woodpecker holes for nesting. The brood size is fairly large, occasionally up to 10, indicating a high juvenile mortality rate. The call is a series of low, fast hoots.

Because the boreal owl is so secretive, it is easily overlooked. Only within the past 15 years was it discovered in the central Rockies, and diligent searchers have now found it in New Mexico. It seems likely that this shy bird lives in other pockets of alpine forest habitat, out of sight – and knowledge – of humans.

IDENTIFICATION

PLUMAGE: Squarish, tuftless head, heavy black borders around light facial discs, white breast streaked with brown, brown back spotted with white. Bill yellow or white.

DISTRIBUTION: Boreal forests from Canadian Maritimes to Alaska, south in Rockies; presumably to New Mexico and Arizona in mountains.

FOOD: Small mammals and birds.

NEST: Tree cavities.

EGGS: 4–6; white.

SAW-WHET OWL
AEGOLIUS ACADICUS

The saw-whet's unusual name comes from one of its equally unusual calls which sounds like someone sharpening the teeth on a saw. In this modern age such a rural simile may only confuse most people, so suffice it to say that the call is short and raspy – and not heard as often as the saw-whet's more common note, a series of endlessly repeated mechanical whistles.

The saw-whet is the southern counterpart to the boreal owl, very similar in appearance but a shade smaller in size, with a rustier cast overall. It has a strange distribution pattern – up the Appalachians to the Northeast and upper Midwest, across southern

Canada, along the Pacific coast from Alaska south, and over the West except for the most arid deserts. It is a year-round resident in most of its range, although some birds (probably juveniles) migrate into the Plains and the South. A separate population is also resident in the highlands of central Mexico.

In the U.S. and Canada, the saw-whet inhabits coniferous woods and mixed deciduous-coniferous forests, although it has shown a fair degree of flexibility in habitat choice, and has been found breeding in pure hardwood stands.

The saw-whet is a mouser, and considering this bird's small size (about 8 inches) a white-footed mouse is formidable game. The owl's talons are tiny but extremely sharp, however, and they do the job. Insects and small birds like chickadees are also taken, which explains the vehemence with which songbirds will scold a saw-whet they find roosting during the day. The smaller birds are safe, for the owl does its hunting at night, when it has the advantage of silence and surprise.

Saw-whets take over old woodpecker holes for nesting, and like screech-owls they respond well to the offer of artificial nest boxes; for either species the box should be about 16 inches deep, with a three-inch entrance hole and a layer of sawdust in the bottom. Juvenile saw-whets are dark brown above and solid chestnut below, with prominent white eyebrows.

IDENTIFICATION

PLUMAGE: Reddish facial discs without black borders, reddish streaking on breast, back rusty brown with white large white spots.

DISTRIBUTION: Mixed or coniferous forests in West, southern Canada, Northeast and Appalachians; also winters in Plains woodlands, parts of South.

FOOD: Small mammals, some birds and insects.

NEST: Tree cavity or artificial nest box.

EGGS: 4–6; white.

APPENDIX
Selected Refuges and Organizations

Most hawk-watches are known to relatively few people, but some have achieved international recognition. Some of the best:

Hawk Mountain Sanctuary. The world's first refuge for birds of prey was established in 1934 along eastern Pennsylvania's Kittatinny Ridge. Peak hawk migration is September-November, but the 2,000-acre, privately owned sanctuary is open year-round, with a visitors center, hiking trails and educational programs. For more information contact Hawk Mountain Sanctuary Association, Route 2, Kempton, Pa, 19529.

Cape May Bird Observatory. Cape May is a magnet for migrants of all types, from songbirds and hawks to owls, herons and shorebirds. A hawk-watch platform near the lighthouse is manned by the CMBO through the fall, but the migration can be observed at many locations, including the South Cape May Meadows (a Nature Conservancy property) and Higbee Beach. Cape May Bird Observatory, P.O. Box 3, Cape May Point, N.J. 08212.

Braddock Bay on New York's Lake Ontario shoreline is one of the best spots in the East for spring hawk-watching, particularly for red-shouldered hawks in March. Braddock Bay Raptor Research, 432 Manitou Beach Rd., Hilton, N.Y. 14468, is a private organization that conducts the counts.

The **Golden Gate Raptor Observatory** in California conducts spring and fall hawk-watches in the Marin Headlands near San Francisco. GGRO, Building 204, Ft. Mason, San Francisco, Calif., 94123.

The **Snake River Birds of Prey Area,** 30 miles south of Boise, Idaho, holds more than 600 breeding pairs of 15 species of raptors, a denser concentration than anywhere else in the world. The 480,000-acre refuge is owned by the federal Bureau of Land Management (BLM). For more information, write: Snake River Birds of Prey Area, BLM, 3948 Development Ave., Boise, ID 83705.

The **Hawk Migration Association of North America** is a coalition of serious hawk-watchers and biologists that tabulates migratory data from across the U.S. and Canada. For information, write HMANA at Box 51, Washington, Conn. 06793.

RIGHT Eastern Screech-Owl

RIGHT Gyrfalcon

Selected Reading

There are many field guides on the market, some good, some not so good. Two of the best for general birding, which include excellent sections on raptors, are:

A Field Guide to the Birds (Eastern and Western editions), Roger Tory Peterson, Houghton Mifflin Co.

Field Guide to the Birds of North America, published by the National Geographic Society.

For more advanced birders:
The Audubon Society Master Guide to Birding (three volumes), edited by John Farrand Jr. and published by Alfred A. Knopf Co. Devotes two or more pages to each species, with good coverage of raptors.

Hawks, by William S. Clark and illustrated by Brian K. Wheeler, is one of the Peterson Field Guide series. It covers all North American diurnal raptors in great detail, with excellent paintings that show all ages and color phases, and extensive accompanying text. Houghton Mifflin Co., 1987.

Hawks in Flight, by Pete Dunne, with illustrations by David Sibley and photos by Clay Sutton (Houghton Mifflin 1988) is not a field guide, but a thoughtful, eminently readable work on identifying hawks through the subtle clues of behaviour and form.

INDEX

ACKNOWLEDGMENTS
AND PICTURE CREDITS

The author and publishers would like to thank Doug Wechsler at VIREO for organizing the provision of the photographs in the book, including the work of the following:

J R Woodward: pp 7, 63, 72 right; B K Wheeler: pp 8, 9, 15 bottom, 17, 18, 21, 24, 25, 31, 38, 41, 45, 46, 47, 50, 51, 52, 53, 54, 58, 60, 64, 68, 75; F K Schleicher: pp 8, 16, 19; D & M Zimmerman: pp 10, 71, 73 left, 74, 79, 81, 83, 91; H Cruikshank: pp 11, 28, 33, 39, 70, 72 left; P McLain: p12; D Roby: pp 13, 15 top, 78, 90; N G Smith: p14; A Morris: p20; S Lafrance: p27; N Abel: p29; S J Lane: pp 30, 55; I Melliger: p32; S Holt: p34; A Carey: pp 35, 36, 37, 56; H Ericsson: p42; D R Herr: p44; W Greene: p49; R Ballou: pp 57, 82; W S Clark: p59; C Munn: p61; C R Sams 11: p62 top; J Oakley: p62 bottom; M P Kahl: p65; J Olsen: p66; F Lantins: p67; J Ruos: p69; S Fried: p73 right; T Fitzharris: p76; B Henry: p77; J Dunning: p80; T Zurowski: pp 84, 85; B Lipschutz: p86; S Bahrt: p87; B Sadsby: p88; J P Myers: p89.